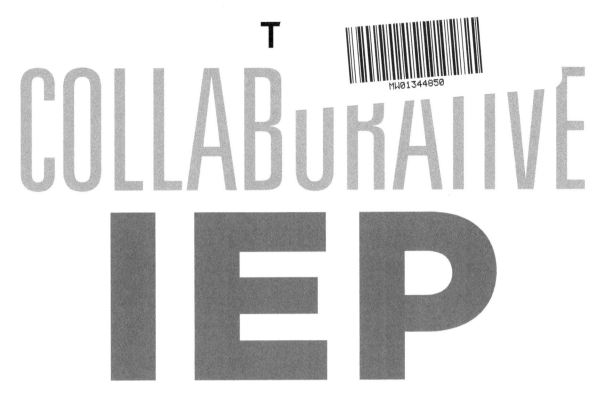

COLLABORATIVE IEP

Working Together for LIFE-CHANGING Special Education

Kristen M. Bordonaro   **Megan Clarke**

Foreword by Julie A. Schmidt

Solution Tree | Press
a division of Solution Tree

Copyright © 2025 by Solution Tree Press

Materials appearing here are copyrighted. With one exception, all rights are reserved. Readers may reproduce only those pages marked "Reproducible." Otherwise, no part of this book may be reproduced or transmitted in any form or by any means (electronic, photocopying, recording, or otherwise) without prior written permission of the publisher.

555 North Morton Street
Bloomington, IN 47404
800.733.6786 (toll free) / 812.336.7700
FAX: 812.336.7790

email: info@SolutionTree.com
SolutionTree.com

Visit **go.SolutionTree.com/specialneeds** to download the free reproducibles in this book.

Printed in the United States of America

Library of Congress Cataloging-in-Publication Data
Names: Bordonaro, Kristen M., author. | Clarke, Megan, author.
Title: The collaborative IEP : working together for life-changing special
    education / Kristen M. Bordonaro, Megan Clarke.
Description: Bloomington, IN : Solution Tree Press, 2024. | Includes
    bibliographical references and index.
Identifiers: LCCN 2024030937 (print) | LCCN 2024030938 (ebook) | ISBN
    9781958590157 (paperback) | ISBN 9781958590164 (ebook)
Subjects: LCSH: Special education teachers--Professional relationships. |
    Teaching teams. | Individualized education programs.
Classification: LCC LC3969 .B67 2024 (print) | LCC LC3969 (ebook) | DDC
    371.9--dc23/eng/20240808
LC record available at https://lccn.loc.gov/2024030937
LC ebook record available at https://lccn.loc.gov/2024030938

Solution Tree
Jeffrey C. Jones, CEO
Edmund M. Ackerman, President

Solution Tree Press
President and Publisher: Douglas M. Rife
Associate Publishers: Todd Brakke and Kendra Slayton
Editorial Director: Laurel Hecker
Art Director: Rian Anderson
Copy Chief: Jessi Finn
Senior Production Editor: Sarah Foster
Proofreader: Sarah Ludwig
Text and Cover Designer: Rian Anderson
Acquisitions Editor: Hilary Goff
Assistant Acquisitions Editor: Elijah Oates
Content Development Specialist: Amy Rubenstein
Associate Editor: Sarah Ludwig
Editorial Assistant: Anne Marie Watkins

Acknowledgments

The authors would like to thank the following people.

- To our students and their families, we thank you for always being our biggest teachers.
- To our staff, colleagues, mentors, and professional partners, we thank you for your trust, your thoughts, and your willingness to join us on this journey.
- To our families, we love you and appreciate you more than we could ever show. Thank you for your support, your grace, your time, and your understanding.

Solution Tree Press would like to thank the following reviewers:

Courtney Andre
Special Education Teacher
Pella High School
Pella, Iowa

Doug Crowley
Assistant Principal
DeForest Area High School
DeForest, Wisconsin

Louis Lim
Principal
Bur Oak Secondary School
Markham, Ontario, Canada

Kory Taylor
Reading Interventionist
Arkansas Virtual Academy
Little Rock, Arkansas

Sheryl Walters
Senior School Assistant Principal
Calgary, Alberta, Canada

Vist **go.SolutionTree.com/specialneeds** to download the free reproducibles in this book.

Table of Contents

Reproducible pages are in italics.

About the Authors ix

Foreword xi

INTRODUCTION   **Our Whys** 1
    Megan's Why 3
    Kristen's Why 4
    Importance of Life-Changing IEPs 6
    How This Book Is Organized 7

PART 1   The Why   11

CHAPTER 1   **Discovering Why Collaborative IEPs Are Essential** 13
    Starting With Public Law 94-142 15
    Learning About *Endrew F. v. Douglas County* 16
    Exploring Special Education Post–*Endrew F.* 17
    Understanding Why General Education Should Be Considered First 17
    Learning Why Interventions Are Essential 20
    Conclusion 22
    Chapter 1 Reflection 23

CHAPTER 2   **Taking a Collaborative Approach** 25
    Understanding Essential Versus Nice-to-Know Standards 27
    Identifying Priority Standards 28
    Aligning for Alternative Assessments 30
    Conclusion 31
    Chapter 2 Reflection 31

CHAPTER 3 Including Parents and Guardians as Partners in the IEP Process ... 33

Scheduling the IEP Meeting ... 35
Making Participation Meaningful ... 36
Using PATH and MAPS for Person-Centered Planning ... 37
Getting Input From Private Providers ... 38
Timing the Drafting of the Proposed IEP ... 39
Conclusion ... 40
Chapter 3 Reflection ... 41
Family IEP Input ... *42*
Private Provider Planning Collaboration Tool ... *44*

PART 2 The How 45

CHAPTER 4 Writing the PLAAFP Statement ... 47

Components of the PLAAFP ... 48
Starting With Strengths ... 48
Academic Achievement ... 51
Functional Performance ... 52
Conclusion ... 54
Chapter 4 Reflection ... 55
Teacher PLAAFP Input Document ... *56*
Team Feedback Form ... *58*

CHAPTER 5 Writing Goals: Getting Started ... 61

Kristen's Travel Analogy ... 61
Megan's Travel Analogy ... 62
Writing IEP Goals ... 62
Considering Two Critical Questions for Goals ... 64
Writing Goals as a Team ... 64
Writing Goals as an Individual ... 69
Conclusion ... 71
Chapter 5 Reflection ... 72

CHAPTER 6 Writing Goals: Data Considerations 73
Writing the Present Level of Performance 74
Determining When to Use Benchmarks or Objectives 78
Finalizing the Writing of Life-Changing Goals 80
Implementing Goal Data Collection 80
Using the Critical Questions of a PLC 81
Conclusion 82
Chapter 6 Reflection 83

CHAPTER 7 Understanding Accommodations and Modifications 85
Exploring Accommodations and Modifications 85
Using Data to Inform Accommodations and Modifications ... 88
Conclusion 91
Chapter 7 Reflection 91

CHAPTER 8 Determining Service Minutes and Placement 93
Connecting Least Restrictive Environment and Service Minutes ... 94
Determining the Best Location for Services 96
Conclusion 99
Chapter 8 Reflection 100

CHAPTER 9 Exploring Behavior, Assistive Tech, Transition, and Low Incidence 101
Behavior 101
Assistive Technology 103
Low-Incidence Disabilities 105
Related Services Within Low Incidence 107
Transition Services 107
Conclusion 108
Chapter 9 Reflection 108

Epilogue 109

APPENDIX A **Examples of PLAAFPs and Goals** 111
    Early Childhood. 111
    Early Elementary 112
    Late Elementary 113
    Middle School 114
    High School. 116
    Post–High School Transition 117

APPENDIX B **Collaborative IEPs: Current Reality, Identifying Essential Actions, and Action Steps** 119
    Red, Yellow, and Green Light Areas *120*

References and Resources 121

Index. 127

About the Authors

Kristen M. Bordonaro has served as a school and district-level administrator for the last fifteen years. She has experience working with both private and public school districts as well as special education collaboratives. Most recently, she served as director of programs and services for the Exceptional Learners Collaborative in Buffalo Grove, Illinois.

Kristen's knowledge and background in leading professional learning communities (PLCs) have allowed teams to truly understand the connection between PLC practices and their direct impact on student growth. She guides the process of understanding the standards through implementing specially designed instruction with measurable and meaningful individualized education plans (IEPs). She has spent the past few years working with districts to deepen their understanding of general and special education, working collaboratively to identify areas of strength and improvement within their service delivery models. Kristen's passion is in uniting school teams to support the needs of all students through an "all means all" model.

In her career as an educator, Kristen has served as a classroom teacher, special education classroom teacher, resource teacher, building leader, program manager, and district office administrator. She has supported all grade levels, from early childhood through transition programming.

Kristen earned her bachelor's degree in elementary education from Trinity International University. She also holds master's degrees in special education and educational leadership, as well as an educational specialist degree in educational leadership, from Western Illinois University. Kristen completed her doctorate at Aurora University, focusing her dissertation on the *Endrew F.* case and how children and school districts have been impacted by this landmark decision.

 **Megan Clarke** is the superintendent of a special education collaborative serving four school districts in Illinois: Adlai E. Stevenson District 125, Kildeer Countryside Community Consolidated School District 96, Lincolnshire–Prairie View School District 103, and Fox Lake School District 114.

Megan has more than twenty-five years of experience in education, having served as an assistant superintendent of pupil services and bilingual services, a director of special education, a principal, an assistant principal, and a special education teacher.

She also served on a transformation team for a state takeover district in Illinois. During her tenure with the district, Megan made significant changes in special education and general education supports that allowed the district to close more than fifteen state findings.

In another role, Megan collaborated with neighboring school districts to build classrooms for students with significant needs, allowing students to attend schools with typical peers within their own school communities.

Megan also serves on the board of the Illinois Alliance of Administrators of Special Education and cochairs the federal committee.

Megan earned a bachelor's degree in speech and language pathology from the University of Arkansas, an educational specialist degree in leadership from Northern Illinois University, and two master's degrees in special education and administration from National Louis University.

To book Kristen M. Bordonaro and Megan Clarke for professional development, contact pd@SolutionTree.com.

Foreword

By Julie A. Schmidt

Whatever winding path you are on, either personally or professionally, you sometimes come together with people you were meant to be with to accomplish something meaningful. *Yes We Can!* (Friziellie, Schmidt, & Spiller, 2016) and *The Collaborative IEP* are the results of passionate professionals realizing life-changing work needs to be done and that work can only be done together.

Kristen M. Bordonaro, Megan Clarke, Jeanne Spiller, Heather Friziellie, and I all had the privilege of leading together in Kildeer Countryside Community Consolidated School District 96 in the suburbs of Chicago in different roles and at various times over the last nineteen years. District 96 began its professional learning community (PLC) journey in 2001, and soon, many of the practices were becoming deeply rooted in the professional culture of the district. During that time, special educators became members of grade-level and content teams, and something incredible happened! Teachers reported that students entitled to special education services were engaging in their learning at higher levels, and adults were beginning to define *advocacy* in new ways. By the end of 2008, a benchmarking study showed that the district was leading the state in terms of closing the gaps between all students and students entitled to special education services. What were we doing differently? We were taking collective ownership of the learning of all students and engaging in PLC practices to ensure that access to rigor was universal.

As students progressed, the sense of urgency around *all* students benefiting from best practices grew exponentially. This urgency led to the district's withdrawal from a large county special education cooperative so that it could design a more local cooperative dedicated to ensuring that high-leverage and life-changing services were available to all our students with identified disabilities. Kristen Bordonaro worked tirelessly to ensure that our most challenged students had access not only to a neighborhood learning environment but also to rigor. Today, Megan Clarke serves as the superintendent of the special education collaborative we designed, and they both share their experience and expertise with educators across the United States. Imagine how grateful all five of us were to have found leaders with whom we shared a very specific passion for shifting traditional special education practices to ensure access to rigor for all students, regardless of the adverse effects of their disabilities!

While we celebrate the incredible progress in our district, across the United States, we often hear questions regarding what the role of special education is in a PLC, what general and special educators should be collaborating on, and what role, if any, the general educator should play in the creation and implementation of the individualized education program (IEP) for students. This book provides clarity on these critical issues.

The Collaborative IEP: Working Together for Life-Changing Special Education is driven by the fundamental belief that all students can learn at high levels, regardless of the challenges they face due to the adverse effects of their disability. It underscores a powerful shift in educational practice—moving from isolated efforts to a collaborative approach that leverages the strengths and expertise of both general and special educators. This paradigm shift is not merely about meeting compliance or fulfilling legal mandates; it is about transforming lives through intentional, collective action. We believe that this is the way it was always meant to be, but over time, silos occurred, and the walls of those silos became difficult to dismantle.

Traditionally, the development of IEPs often has been relegated to special education professionals, working in silos and addressing isolated aspects of a student's needs. However, this approach leads to fragmented learning experiences that fail to capture the student's holistic potential and limits their access to content expertise and rigor. Therefore, the challenge is to ensure that general and special educators work hand in hand, creating a seamless, integrated support system that promotes rigorous academic achievement and meaningful progress toward individualized goals.

The belief that all kids can learn at high levels is not simply an ideal; it is a call to action for educators to hold themselves and their students to the highest expectations. When we adopt this mindset, we transform our approach to teaching and learning, ensuring that every student has access to the rich, rigorous curriculum that prepares them for success in school and beyond.

The foundation of an effective IEP is built on a deep understanding of the student's current levels of performance, both academically and functionally. This understanding requires the collaborative effort of a multidisciplinary team, including general education teachers, special education teachers, related service providers, and family members. Each team member brings a unique perspective and expertise that, when combined, creates a comprehensive picture of the student's strengths and areas of need. This collective insight is critical in crafting goals that are not only standards aligned but also tailored to the individual needs of the student, ensuring that they are ambitious and life altering.

A collaborative IEP requires the alignment of instructional strategies and supports across all settings. In too many cases, students experience disjointed learning as they move between different classrooms and service providers, each focusing on separate goals or standards. This compartmentalized approach can hinder a student's ability to generalize and apply skills in varied contexts. By contrast, a collaborative team works together to create a cohesive learning experience, where strategies are reinforced and integrated throughout the school day. This unified approach maximizes every opportunity for the student to practice and master critical skills, leading to more significant and sustained progress.

Moreover, collaboration extends beyond the school walls to include families as essential partners in the IEP process. Parents and guardians offer invaluable insights into their child's unique needs, preferences, and experiences. Their active involvement ensures that the IEP reflects the student's holistic context, bridging the gap between home and school. Effective communication and partnership with families are paramount, as they provide continuity and support vital for the student's success.

As you embark on this journey through *The Collaborative IEP*, we invite you to embrace the mindset that every student can achieve at high levels. Recognize that the strength of an IEP lies in the collective effort and shared commitment of the entire team. By working together, you can and will create educational experiences that are empowering and life-changing for your students. This book is more than a guide; it is a call to action for educators to come together, break down silos, and build a future where all students can reach their full potential.

In this book, Kristen and Megan share insights and strategies that will inspire you to reimagine your approach to special education. May this book serve as a catalyst for change, fostering a culture of collaboration and high expectations that will transform the educational landscape for students with disabilities.

Julie A. Schmidt has been a school psychologist, assistant director of special education, director of student services, assistant superintendent for student services, and superintendent of schools and has served at both the high school and elementary school levels over her thirty-three-year career as an educator. She served on the board of directors for the Illinois Association of School Administrators and as president of the executive board of the Exceptional Learners Collaborative.

INTRODUCTION

Our Whys

We (Megan and Kristen) have worked for more than a decade to support school teams in building their capacity to create the most substantial individualized education plans (IEPs) for their students, grow in their capacity to support students, become more intentional, continuously raise the bar of expectations, and carry the banner for advancing the field of special education. Our priority is for collaborative teams to create student-centered IEPs, using a continuum of services that supports the student and allows for fluidity throughout the student's day. As an overarching goal, we believe students are best supported through a team of educators who share the collective responsibility of creating life-changing educational opportunities where we always presume competence and that *all* students learn at the highest levels. We also want to empower a community of passionate educators who want to change the world by supporting high learning expectations for all students. Finally, we want to equip teams to feel confident in supporting students' individual needs and to continuously challenge their thoughts on what is best in the education field.

Across the United States, educators come to work each day to support students' exceptional learning needs. With that desire comes goodwill, good intentions, and doing the best we can with what we have to create a learning environment where we provide a safe and meaningful educational experience for our students. We know that our students have unique learning needs, operating within the scope of our districts and our own understanding of how to help students learn, and hoping we make the right decisions. However, as the saying goes, "Hope is not a strategy." The United States Supreme Court affirmed in the *Endrew F.* decision that students with disabilities must be given more than minimal education benefits; therefore, we can no longer hope that we are making a difference. Instead, we have a moral and ethical responsibility to *ensure* students are learning at the highest levels, in *their* least restrictive environment at all times. As members of professional learning communities (PLCs), we can agree on the power of educators working collaboratively, building collective efficacy, and sharing ownership of student learning. Student IEP teams consist of educators who support the student, general education teachers, special education teachers, related service personnel, families, and school administration working together toward the same outcomes; sharing the ownership of planning, learning, and growth; and supporting one another. Working together, the goals of these collaborative teams are to increase opportunities for generalization and reinforcement of skills and collaborative problem solving while trying to provide students with ways to demonstrate their learning and independently access grade-level general education content.

The opposite of collaborative teams owning the student's learning is a single or silo setting. These settings support individual student skills in isolation, with each team member working on their activities and lacking the integration of supporting the student across their school day. In silo settings, a special education teacher may be working on specific skills or strategies aligned to a specific IEP goal, while a general education teacher is working on a different set of skills or strategies aligned toward grade-level standards. A related service member may focus on something different within their area of expertise. The student may be learning from each individual, but their learning is often disjointed throughout their school day. For a student, this can limit the opportunities to display their skill if everyone is working on something different. Often, it can become difficult for the student to generalize their skills when they are taught these skills in compartmentalized efforts. For example, a student may learn a specific strategy in mathematics problem solving within general education. Then, their special education teacher may teach the student about telling elapsed time on clock faces. Therefore, the student stopped thinking about their newly learned mathematics problem-solving strategies from their earlier class because they started focusing on the skill of telling time. This type of service delivery model allows a student to make some progress; however, it may be much slower progress because new learning gaps emerge when the student tries to focus on different skills simultaneously. In some ways, it feels like the game of *Whac-a-Mole*, where teachers address skills as they pop up instead of building a collective foundation of skills.

In a collaborative team service model, every individual on the student's team considers themselves to be the teacher with responsibility for student learning and growth. Therefore, general education teachers, special education teachers, interventionists, special area teachers, and related service providers plan together, share strategies and goal areas, and provide comprehensive support to the student as a whole. Likewise, in the earlier example of problem solving in general education mathematics, when the general education teacher and special education teacher plan together on the strategies, they will both reinforce and interweave the understanding of elapsed time through the problem-solving strategies. When we are co-planning to co-serve the student, we share strategies, expectations, vocabulary, and repeated opportunities to reinforce the learning concepts and opportunities for the student to demonstrate their learning. Collaborative teams promote the expertise of all members of our team: the general education teacher who is a grade-level content specialist; the special education teacher who is an instructional strategist of students' individual needs due to how their disability impacts them; interventionist who may have expertise or knowledge in a specific content area or tool; special area teachers who have the unique opportunity to provide instruction in a variety of settings such as music, physical education, art, or STEM; related service members with their language, motor, or social-emotional lens; and families who are student specialists and know their child best. When we all work together for the same end goal, we create the most intentional experiences across the student's school day, maximizing every instructional opportunity for the student to learn at high levels.

Megan's Why

For students identified to receive special education supports, the IEP serves as a roadmap for school teams. Over the combined twenty-five-plus years in education Kristen and I share, we have worked through the good, bad, and ugly of writing and implementing IEPs for students. Through working with many different district and school teams across the United States, we have spent many days and nights helping them understand how to create an IEP that is more than a legal document to measure growth. We want them to know that when an IEP is created with the input of multiple stakeholders, a collaborative team, and a focus on high expectations, it changes the outcome for the student's academic and functional skills.

For some, writing an IEP is a task they only do as a job requirement. Others view an IEP as something the special education team works with or, at worst, as a way to enable students who don't want to work as hard as others. However, a good IEP targets a student's needs and creates a life-changing instructional plan. This structured instruction plan focuses on present levels, specific goal areas, and necessary accommodations. In addition, the IEP provides a service delivery plan directed first at meeting the student's general education needs and then planning how to deliver special education services.

My *why* for this book is personal as well as professional. I spent a lot of time reading textbooks and other required books throughout elementary and middle school because it took me longer than other students to comprehend the text. I could decode the text, but I struggled for years with answering comprehension questions. When I related to the text, it was easier to answer the comprehension questions. However, with abstract text or classic literature, I had to reread it or make up my answers to the comprehension questions. In high school, I studied many hours after school to get good grades, but it took me much longer to read the required texts.

My parents asked my counselor about my homework load and shared my difficulties. After testing, I scored in the average range in all the assessments, except I was slightly weaker in comprehension. My counselor advocated for specialized tutoring to give me the tools for better comprehension and continued pushing me to get good grades. I spent over a year and a half learning those tools while graduating on time with grades of a C or better in all general education high school classes. If I did not have my parents and counselor to advocate for me to get the needed tools, I would not be where I am today as a professional.

After I had an amazing person help me in high school, I wanted to do similar work. I started as a special education teacher to work with students with a specific learning disability. However, my student teaching showed me that I wanted to work with students with significant emotional and behavioral concerns as well as a specific learning disability. During an extended summer school program, I had students with intellectual disabilities, autism, and other complex medical conditions, and I enjoyed that placement. As I continued as a special education self-contained teacher, I learned about collecting data, instructional strategies, and working with paraprofessionals. Still, I needed more exposure to general education to be a more effective practitioner and to understand the whole school atmosphere more in-depth. I realized that we needed to start aligning our goals with the general education standards if we wanted our students to be successful in school and later in life. Therefore, I started partnering more with the general education teachers; however, we needed aligned schedules when we could effectively collaborate.

To make a more significant impact in my work with students, I became a school leader, central office administrator, and now a superintendent of a special education cooperative. Throughout my leadership, I learned special educators can get stuck in the black and white of the law. But it's their job to look at the student and plan for that individual. Kristen and I feel so passionate about this work that we decided to help other special educators by presenting at conferences across the United States and writing this book.

Kristen's Why

IEPs have impacted my professional and personal lives. Throughout all three of my children's education, they have received services at some point. As a parent, sitting on the other side of the table and trying to advocate for creating a plan that will most positively impact my child has been one of my life's most significant challenges. I've had to learn everything from coming to terms with parenting a child through special education to then letting go as my oldest child is legally an adult and technically can make their own decisions. While two of our three children received support for speech services in early elementary school, our oldest received services his entire public education career. One constant concern throughout my parenting journey was how we could make a way forward for our children, regardless of their educational needs.

When our oldest was first found eligible for services the week before his third birthday, I felt a sense of urgency to understand how to support him in school. I will always remember sitting through his evaluation assessments and eligibility meeting and hearing the staff discuss my child. In some ways, it felt like a surreal experience that I was listening to but not living in. As the receiving school team reviewed the continuum with us, I remember thinking, *He has to be in a class with verbal students; he will never learn to talk if no one else is talking around him.* After much discussion and emotion, we decided with our school team that it would be in his best interest to participate in our community school early childhood program with a blended setting of students with various needs and some community peers. Within a few months of schooling, not only was he completely potty trained (bless his teachers and staff), but he began to engage in some language. We truly believe that the help of the early childhood team, including teachers and therapists, set the course for our child's learning opportunities.

Throughout my son's full fourteen-and-a-half years of public schooling, we had many peaks and valleys. But throughout, we always felt we could come to the table to problem solve and decide the next best step. When our son entered middle school, we allowed him to determine if and when he wanted to become part of the meetings and express what was most important to him as an outcome of the meeting. It was vital that his specific concerns were addressed and that his voice for his future was part of the meeting. It didn't mean that we always agreed, but we ensured that he had the opportunity to share his thoughts and concerns with the entire team. By the time this book is published, he will have graduated high school and started college. We would never be where we are now without the support of amazing teachers and therapists and a terrific special education administrator who never stopped supporting our hopes for him.

When I think about sitting on the professional side of the table and the hundreds of IEP meetings I have participated in, I wish I could say with certainty that a life-changing IEP was always created and honored for each student who needed one. However, that is certainly not the case. We are all works in progress, and as the poet Maya Angelou (Quote Investigator, 2022) once said, "You did then what you knew how to do, and when you knew better, you did better." Educators in any healthy school culture continuously strive to improve, do better, and learn and grow, especially within special education. When educators begin to assume competence, they allow students to demonstrate what they know and avoid putting a ceiling on their learning. Therefore, every time you join a student's IEP meeting, remember that you have the privilege and capacity to change the trajectory of their lives for the better. As an IEP team member, each of us has a responsibility to ensure the plan is challenging and individualized. Most importantly, it should align to ensure the student has the opportunity to thrive within the least restrictive environment and outline dedicated steps to increase their intentional learning and participation in each environment.

All means *all*. We know strategies that are helpful for students within special education are typically strategies that benefit all students. When *all* educators embrace the learning of *all* students and create environments designed to the edges of instruction rather than to the middle, we will be able to break down walls that prevent students from accessing environments and truly build an environment that doesn't just say "all means all," but encourages that value to become part of who we are and part of our culture of expectations.

Megan and I used to joke (and still do sometimes) that we would ask families where they see advertising for our districts since many families with students with both high-incidence special education needs and extremely complex special education needs move into our districts. Obviously, we know no company is out there advertising the support students receive in our districts. However, we know that students' needs are increasing, and more students than before are learning within their neighborhood schools. The COVID-19 pandemic and rising mental health needs continue to impact students while access to these supports in the community decreases. Families and school teams are finding it essential to rely on the public school system to meet these increasing needs while also focusing on ensuring academic success. As we embark on this journey together, we encourage you to consider all possibilities, champion individual students, and build a world with endless possibilities for students.

Importance of Life-Changing IEPs

This book focuses on the essential steps for teams to create life-changing IEPs. IEPs are created to have goals written as SMART goals, present levels that demonstrate the student's need, and appropriate team members at the meeting. However, that is different from a team coming together, intentionally planning, and creating an IEP built on the understanding that as a result of the student receiving *this* specially designed instruction, *this* student's life will be changed for the better. IEPs that are life-changing are built by teams committed to working together to provide intentional instruction around the specific areas that will have the greatest impact on *this* student's future: academically, social-emotionally, and functionally. We are working as one collaborative team to prepare students for successful, independent lives as adults. Our role as the student's collaborative team is to provide the strategies and skills necessary for the student to progress and have as many options as possible throughout their education. We must ensure that we are continually working toward independence in adulthood, with opportunities to further their schooling, career, or vocational skills as they desire.

In general education, when teams prioritize and unpack standards, they follow a structure or framework to determine the most essential standards. In *Energize Your Teams*, educators Thomas W. Many, Michael J. Maffoni, Susan K. Sparks, and Tesha Ferriby Thomas (2022) state educators are focusing on the standards that have readiness, endurance, assessment, and leverage (REAL). Teams of educators come together to prioritize these standards as the essentials that we guarantee every student in the grade level will master as a result of instruction. Teams collaborate at length to ensure they focus on the right standards to provide the highest quality education they can for their students. When we consider an IEP to be life-changing, we ensure the goals and standards we are aligning with are also passing that REAL structure. Does this goal have the readiness knowledge and skills for us to spend time on? Is it going to endure throughout the student's school year? Can we measure the growth or assess the support across the student's school day? When we have ensured we are working on the right work, we are aligning specific strategies and skills for the individual student to access the general education curriculum, and we have a plan of how a collaborative team will support this learning, then we have a life-changing IEP. As with all collaborative activities, teams that come together to build a collaborative IEP know the strength of the team is in their interdependence and their collective skills in meeting this child's needs, which means we need the strength and insight of each member of the team working together to achieve the highest outcomes. We know that we need the expertise of the general education teacher in not only building the present levels but also helping to craft a goal that will align with the grade-level expectations while meeting the individual learning needs due to the student's disability. While each team and school may have different structures and types of teachers supporting the student, the essential foundation has the following common understandings.

- All students can learn at high levels.
- Collaborative teams are essential to student success.
- IEPs must be life-changing for the student.

Teams that embrace these three understandings intentionally work together, sharing collaborative planning, intentional instruction, and student growth. These teams ensure they find ways to communicate and plan, be it in person during team times or through shared planning documents where each member contributes to the strategies and data collection within their time frames. The team builds the common understanding that it will not allow time or other factors to prevent collaboration because when we collaborate, everyone benefits.

How This Book Is Organized

Each chapter breaks down IEPs to provide a practical working knowledge of how collaborative teams can create stronger IEPs, leading to more robust instruction and learning. We highlight the essential pieces and encourage teams to use a future-based approach to immediately change their practices to better support students. When we use the word *teams*, we refer to anyone and everyone responsible for the student's growth. While each student's IEP needs will differ, their team consists of individuals supporting their growth and learning. At a minimum, a team should include a general education teacher, a special education teacher, and family members. Then, depending on the student's needs, additional members may be included, such as a speech-language pathologist, occupational therapist, school counselor, interventionist, and so on. The team also consists of any additional teachers the student sees throughout the day such as art, music, or physical education teachers. When working with a student who has an IEP, every member who supports the student has ownership of their IEP, providing input, strengths, weaknesses, strategies, and data toward the student's progress.

Next, let's look at the topics in each chapter. In chapter 1, we go through the history of special education in the United States, especially the landmark *Endrew F. v. Douglas* U.S. Supreme Court case. Then, we explore special education after that decision and discuss why interventions are essential.

In chapter 2, we explore using a collaborative approach to special education that engages all the stakeholders on the school teams. Then, in chapter 3, we explain why partnering with parents and guardians is essential in the IEP process, how to make their participation meaningful, and how to use person-centered planning and scheduling for the IEP process.

In chapter 4, we discuss writing the present levels of academic achievement and functional performance (PLAAFP) statement and its components of students' strengths, academic achievement, and functional performance. In chapters 5 and 6, we discuss writing IEP goals, determining when to use benchmarks or objectives, and using the four critical questions of a PLC at Work®.

In chapter 7, we explore accommodations and modifications and use data to inform them. In chapter 8, we discuss determining service minutes and placement, the least restrictive environment, and the best locations for services.

In chapter 9, we touch on behavior, assistive technology, low incidence and its related services, and transition.

Finally, in appendix A, we provide examples of the PLAAFP and goals for fictional students at every grade level.

Regardless of your role on the IEP team—general education teacher, special education teacher, related service provider, administrator, or parent—we want to simplify the IEP process and provide some practical strategies and structures to demystify how general and special education collaborate to support all learners and create IEPs that are not only compliant but truly a pathway to life-changing education.

At the end of each chapter are reflection topics or thought questions. As you read each section, we wanted to ensure that we paused to reflect on where we are in our journey toward life-changing education. If you are using this book as a book study with your team, we encourage you to use these as opportunities for discussion and action. We have included a reflection reproducible in appendix B to guide the team in identifying where you are currently, and your action steps as a team to move forward.

- **Red light areas:** These areas are mandatory stops! Maybe a hazard is present and must be addressed before moving forward, or take inventory of where you are currently before moving forward. This could be an inventory of mindsets, building structures, or practices that do not align with your beliefs. Before proceeding, ensure you are moving forward, safely, in the right direction. Identifying red light areas is an opportunity to identify your current reality but also to identify practices that must stop now.

- **Yellow light areas:** Slow down and be prepared to stop. These are areas where the current systems and plans may need to be examined to determine where they are taking your team, because it may not be the best direction or may possibly be a detour. You might need to consider your team's paths and possibly recalculate the best route. Yellow light areas are where you identify the essential actions that teams can pursue as they work toward life-changing IEPs.

- **Green light areas:** Green light areas are where you need to continue forward, full speed ahead to reach your goals. Your team has clarity and direction and is ready to hit the highway!

Next, let's look at the history of special education in the United States.

PART 1

THE WHY

CHAPTER 1

DISCOVERING WHY COLLABORATIVE IEPs ARE ESSENTIAL

If a child can't learn the way we teach, maybe we should teach the way they learn.

—Ignacio Estrada

In the introduction, we shared why working in special education is vital to us as professionals and even more so as people. This work is hard. It's emotional for the school teams, the families, and most important, the students. This work is certainly not for the faint of heart or those who are OK with being OK. For those who are willing to challenge the status quo, seek to do more, do better, not accept mediocracy, not listen to naysayers, and come to work every day carrying the banner that every student can learn at high levels, this work can be exhausting. School teams often must do more with less. They step up to the challenge, find ways to support the learning needs of all students, and create meaningful learning experiences for students who receive services. In highly effective schools, every educator in the building sees themselves as a teacher of *all* students. When supporting the learning of a student entitled to services through an IEP, every individual on the IEP team is responsible for the learning and growth of that student. As a team, each person may have their area of expertise; however, they achieve the highest levels of success when working together and understanding how to support one another through the shared ownership of the IEP. As teams build into their interdependence, this book serves as a foundation for all team members: general education teachers, special education teachers, interventionists, related service team members, and families. Understanding how your expertise impacts the team and how each person supports the student through a collective model allows for greater growth as a life-changing team. The student's IEP is a collective responsibility of the team, not to be implemented or owned by one member. Each teacher and staff member within the school who provides instruction to the individual student makes up their team. Likewise, we want every educator who supports students with exceptional learning needs to be a member of the life-changing education team. Students have a variety of individuals responsible for their instruction each day, well beyond a grade-level or content-area general education teacher and special education teacher. While the focus of this book is on the IEP as the backbone, we also believe that every adult who supports students with IEPs can learn and grow from supporting students in a collaborative model. As members of the collaborative team, each team member must understand how the IEP supports students and their role in that support, which goes far beyond answering a few questions to build a present level or receiving a copy of the IEP at the start of the school year.

Schools are more than academics. Successful learning is a vital part of achieving those outcomes and requires recognition that schools are also places for social-emotional learning, mental health counseling, food, and warmth. Students need a place for someone to say their name, to see their friends, and to participate in activities. For some, school serves as their way out of community hardships through scholarships. For others, school serves as students' creative outlet or a place to converse with people who challenge their thoughts.

Unfortunately, when it comes to students who receive identified special education services, the school experience can look very different. Some students who receive these services participate in all the typical general education activities and receive their support embedded throughout the day, and this educational experience continues throughout their school career. For others, school can be the one place families can send their children and feel assured they are safe and cared for throughout the day, which offers a much-needed respite from the additional responsibilities carried by families of students with extensive needs.

According to the U.S. Department of Education's (n.d.) Office of Special Education Programs database, in the 2020–2021 school year, 7.3 million students ages 3–21 received special education services through public school districts. This is approximately 15 percent of all students enrolled in public schools. What is staggering is this number has continued to rise. During the 1990–1991 school year, around 11 percent of students received special education services within the United States (U.S. Department of Education, n.d.).

To understand how we got here, we need to consider the history of special education. We begin with discussing U.S. Public Law 94-142 (GovInfo, 1975), which first mandated special education services in 1975. Then, we move into how that law informs how special education work does not work in schools today. Next, we explore the ramifications of *Endrew F. v. Douglas County* and how that has affected teaching. We discuss why general education should be considered the first and best instruction. Finally, we learn why multitiered system of supports (MTSS) is essential to support the wheels of special education.

Starting With Public Law 94-142

Let's use Public Law 94-142 as our starting point for looking at the history of special education in the United States. In 1975, the U.S. Congress enacted the Education for All Handicapped Children Act (GovInfo, 1975), which began the process of mandating special education services for individuals with identified disabilities. Public Law 94-142 (GovInfo, 1975) had four main purposes.

1. Ensure that all students with disabilities are provided a free appropriate public education (FAPE) in which the student receives special education and related services specific to their needs.

2. Ensure that the rights of students with disabilities and their parents and guardians are protected.

3. Help states and local school districts provide education for *all* students with disabilities.

4. Ensure districts and schools are educating students with disabilities effectively.

Since 1975, the U.S. Congress reauthorized Public Law 94-142 many times and renamed it the Individuals with Disabilities Education Act (IDEA; American Association of School Administrators, 2022). Throughout each revision, Congress added or clarified areas of service and eligibility to improve the lives of individuals with disabilities and to create free appropriate public education for all. While the revisions created more clarity, additional services, or additional specifications for schools, they haven't provided guidance in a few key areas. For example, although the reauthorizations continually added initiative and supports, as of this writing, the U.S. Congress has yet to fully fund these initiatives or emphasize students' growth and potential to exit special education services (American Association of School Administrators, 2022).

Based on data from the U.S. Department of Education's (n.d.) Office of Special Education Programs, between 2011–2012 and 2017–2018, the number of students served under IDEA increased from 6.4 million to 7 million, and the percentage served increased from 13 percent to 14 percent of total public school enrollment. Therefore, in the United States, we are not closing the gap for students and exiting them from special education at the rate that we would have expected. When we consider the concept that students receiving services should be receiving tailored instruction specifically for their individual needs, we would expect to see the number of students requiring services to decrease. We discuss this more in the section, Understanding Why General Education Should Be Considered First (page 17). But first, we discuss the 2017 landmark U.S. Supreme Court case that changed special education.

Learning About *Endrew F. v. Douglas County*

Through due process procedures, districts and families rely on case law that provides interpretation of the IDEA legislation. The *Endrew F. v. Douglas County* U.S. Supreme Court decision shifted how school teams provide special education because the definition of meeting FAPE shifted drastically. Prior to 2017, determining FAPE was primarily based on the *Board of Education v. Rowley* decision.

In *Board of Education v. Rowley* (Library of Congress, 1982), the U.S. Supreme Court provided an interpretation of FAPE that stated districts did not need to maximize a student's education and only needed to implement an IEP that is "reasonably calculated to result in educational benefit." The Court went on to determine that districts were required to provide a "basic floor of opportunity," explaining that schools were not required to provide a Cadillac when a "serviceable Chevy" would suffice, creating the infamous "Chevy not a Cadillac" thought process (Library of Congress, 1982). What did this mean for students? In short, school teams and districts were only required to provide something more to the student with an IEP and did not have to create an IEP designed with maximum benefit for the student.

In 2017's *Endrew F.* decision, the U.S. Supreme Court rejected the *Rowley* minimalist decision and determined it was not in the best interest of students. It created a new definition of how to determine if FAPE has been met (Supreme Court of the United States, 2017). This decision states that school teams are required to create IEPs that allow a student to make "progress appropriate in light of the child's circumstances" and that "every child should have the chance to meet challenging objectives" (U.S. Department of Education, 2017a). Therefore, the Court created a ruling that means that *every* student should have the chance to not just learn but meet *challenging* objectives. Every student. Not only students in general education. Not only students who listen and follow classroom expectations. *Every* student must have the opportunity to learn at high levels that are *challenging*. The Court stated that "any review of an IEP must consider whether the IEP is reasonably calculated to ensure such progress, not whether it would be considered ideal" (U.S. Department of Education, 2017a, p. 5).

With this ruling, the special education world took the first steps to be held to a higher standard of action and responsibility when it came to student growth. School teams can no longer live under a minimalist approach and be safe from due process because they provided *something* to the student. They have to implement an IEP that is *challenging* for *every* student and *reasonably calculated* to *ensure* this growth occurs.

Exploring Special Education Post-*Endrew F.*

Until 2017, school teams were not held as accountable for individual student growth on their IEP goals due to the previous court decisions. Teams were (and still are) required to report to families about the student's growth toward meeting IEP goals each reporting period and annual review time. Concern about a student's lack of growth often results in an increase in special education services or placement in a more restrictive setting. The understanding is that a lack of growth or progress indicates that not enough support exists for the student to make progress.

Even post–*Endrew F.*, school teams are more likely to increase special education services and types of support when a student isn't demonstrating growth rather than reviewing how instruction is delivered or the methodology used. In many cases, if a student is not making the expected progress or continues to struggle with a goal or skill, the team will intervene and increase the amount or type of support the student is receiving instead of looking at why the student is struggling or examining the instruction for possible options to present it another way for the student (Mattos et al., 2025).

School teams frequently look to provide these additional service delivery minutes outside of the general education classroom through alternative tools or boxed programs that may be poorly aligned to general education standards, essentially creating an even larger academic gap for the students to close because now they are missing new instruction. While alternative curriculum boxed programs have a place in the education system, they do not replace the teacher and are only tools rather than a one-size-fits-all solution. Within special education, the students all have unique learning needs and deserve to have specially designed instruction based on those needs rather than following a program lockstep. In addition, based on the student needs and caseload of the special education teacher, the teacher may require access to a variety of tools and curriculum options to effectively meet the goals and needs of their caseload. It isn't uncommon for a special education teacher to have four or more reading or mathematics curriculum boxes because they use different aspects of each based on the unique needs of their students.

Understanding Why General Education Should Be Considered First

All students are considered general education students first. Teams often share this as their mission or beliefs, not only because it is where the special education continuum begins, but also because our goal within the broad field of special education is to have independent access to the general education curriculum. Across the United States, educators often see special education services as a place for students to go when they aren't learning as quickly as others. In our experience, meetings across districts may heavily focus on classroom or grade-level teachers (or special area teachers in art, music, or physical education) bringing their concerns regarding the student's skills or growth to the problem-solving team, and the team rescuing the student and relieving the teacher of the instruction, allowing them to continue to move forward with the remainder of the class. Once a student begins to receive intervention or special education services, they are perceived to be the sole responsibility of the interventionist or special education teacher, resulting in the general education teacher taking less ownership of the student's instruction, academic growth, and day-to-day learning. Teams may begin to accept a student with reduced progress as being OK because they receive support. However, we need students to make relentless progress with the *entire team* owning the concept of content mastery. This team begins with the general education teacher who collaborates with the intervention or special education team on instruction for the student to demonstrate their learning.

When a student struggles to demonstrate their knowledge regularly, we've seen teams remove or increase their time away from core instruction in their grade-level classroom and from the expert content instruction of their grade-level teacher. The result is that the student misses this vital learning time to engage in the same activities as their class and have the same practice opportunities as their peers. They also miss time to engage in natural conversations with peers, learn alongside them, observe how others are thinking, or solve and talk through a problem with a grade-level peer in their classroom setting. As teachers, we want to support students, and our first inclination is often to pull the student to a smaller setting where we can give more individualized instruction or a different skill for them to be successful. However, that is comparable to learning to drive a car by riding a bike in your driveway without any obstacles. The experience is entirely different. It's time to reverse the trend where IEP teams consider general education last when they begin to consider services and provide special education instruction in a separate location using different materials than the general education classroom. Effective intervention programs, such as response to intervention (RTI), are clear in the need to accelerate learning for students who are missing essential grade-level skills without compromising their access to core grade- or course-level instruction (Mattos et al., 2025).

In addition, school teams and families spend countless hours in IEP meetings to determine eligibility, goals, accommodations, and service plans. IEPs help to fulfill the legal requirements to educate a student by providing targeted goals, specific accommodations, special education service minutes, and educational placement for the student.

When you consider the concept that first and best instruction is delivered within the general education setting, we need to consider working collaboratively as IEP teams to create individualized learning experiences for students to be able to access that instruction within general education and support students' needs and to learn in the most natural setting of the classroom (Goodwin, 2022). This shift in providing special education services starts with teams creating IEPs based on the individual needs of the students and on the priority grade-level standards, and describing how to provide this instruction through strategies and skills within the larger school environment.

Special education does have a continuum of services provided through IDEA (2004), and that continuum is a vital part of the work within special education. Figure 1.1 shows the continuum of services and how a student's needs can range from general education with some support to needing highly specialized care in a separate facility.

General education with no support	General education with some support	General education with some support outside of general education	General education with more support outside of general education	General education with extensive support outside of general education	Special education classroom within general education school	Public or therapeutic day school	Hospitalization or residential setting
100 percent general education	100 percent general education	80 percent general education	40 to 79 percent or more general education	Less than 40 percent general education	100 percent special education setting	100 percent special education–alternative setting	100 percent special education–alternative setting

Source: Adapted from IDEA, 2004.

Figure 1.1: Example of the continuum of services.

However, special education teams need to consider the continuum throughout the student's individual day. They need to focus primarily on the student's individual strengths and use those strengths to create an educational plan designed to *intentionally* close the student's learning gap through collaborative teams working together with a steadfast dedication to shared ownership of student learning.

When the entire team takes collective ownership of a student's learning, it allows for a shift for the student. The general education teacher and the special education team become one unit that collaborates across all areas of the student's day to allow for multiple opportunities to demonstrate growth, receive instruction, and embed the general education priority standards within the student's instructional plan. Collaborative ownership between general education and special education for intentional student growth provides the core content knowledge of the general education teacher to be at the center of the student's instruction, creating the foundation on which special education builds instructional strategies to access this vital foundation.

In *Ruthless Equity*, educational consultant Ken Williams (2022) shares that "if we never get around to envisioning a future that's better than our current reality, our efforts in any endeavor will fall short of the mark" (p. 7). Our current reality in special education is not the reality we want for our students. While we may be further along than we were in 2014, our future can be so much brighter. Our students deserve to have us advocate relentlessly to provide rigorous instruction tailored to their individual needs. They deserve to have their educational teams shift the narrative from what they can't do to what they can do through strengths-based IEPs that meet the *Endrew F.* standard of appropriately ambitious and challenging goals and objectives. Our students deserve to have IEP teams be a little nervous about how challenging the goals will be for the student, and that little bit of anxiety about an IEP will stretch the student as well as the team. Students deserve IEPs that are not just legal documents designed to close a gap. They deserve an IEP that changes their life for the better and crafts a different path for them that is beyond anyone's current reality.

Learning Why Interventions Are Essential

Every school has a system in place to provide intervention when students are not making the progress we expect. Often, this is referred to as tiered intervention in response to intervention or multitiered system of supports. These practices allow teams to identify which students are responding to core instruction as expected and identify students who are not making expected progress. Further, teams then use benchmark and classroom data to identify students for targeted intervention, with the goal supposedly to prevent students from requiring extensive special education services. We can assess how students are performing in their core instruction and, when necessary, in supported intervention using the RTI or MTSS process. These are analogous to each other and can typically be referred to interchangeably. When we think about the number of students who receive specialized services, it's important to think of it as similar to a funnel or downward triangle as shown in the RTI at Work™ pyramid (figure 1.2).

The goal is for all students to receive solid core instruction and classroom strategies. Across the school year, some students will need to have a problem-solving process and interventions to grow. Fewer students will be recommended for an initial evaluation or a three-year reevaluation and even fewer students will be found eligible. Figure 1.3 shows the continuum of services and the elements of an IEP.

Discovering Why Collaborative IEPs Are Essential

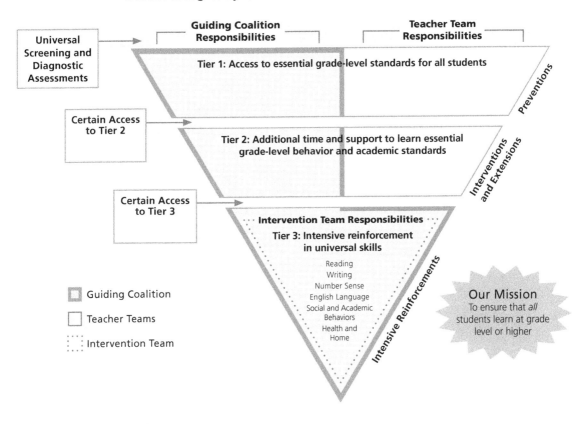

Source: Mattos et al., 2025, p. 12.

Figure 1.2: The RTI at Work pyramid.

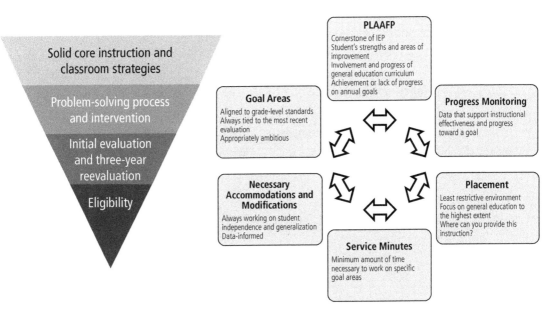

Figure 1.3: Elements of IEP.

Another way to think about it is if your vehicle's low fuel light came on, you wouldn't instantly go to a repair shop or the dealership and ask for a new engine; the first step is to check your fuel level and get more fuel. MTSS can serve as preventive maintenance when all students' growth is regularly reviewed by assessments. Reviewing students' growth toward priority standards ensures that their growth is appropriate. MTSS allows for the opportunity to take a look at all students and identify any who may need support or interventions.

Each state and even each district varies in their implementation of interventions and their special education referral process. What is most important for all teams to consider is that when the MTSS process determines something more specific is occurring that requires additional support, school teams can begin to provide this support and intervention in the specific areas for the student. Grade-level and school teams consisting of grade-level or content teachers, interventionists, and special education teachers must consider data from within the school and any available outside resources, such as private evaluation or diagnosis, when considering how to best support the student. This will guide decision making about when tiered intervention is the better approach and when an evaluation for special education services is the better option. When pursuing an intervention approach, teams must consider all options for how to intervene. If, after exhausting these efforts and general education resources, a student has not yet made the growth that the teams need to see, an evaluation can be conducted to further determine if there is a specific area of disability to support.

Conclusion

Supporting the learning of all students can be a complex yet rewarding journey for school teams. As classroom educators continue to expand their strategies and support the learning of more students within the general education setting, it is imperative to work together in collaborative teams to address the range of learning and design instructional opportunities that meet the needs of all learners. The skills being addressed through a solid core or Tier 1 instruction, MTSS systems, and throughout special education are best addressed by a team of dedicated individuals who believe that all students can learn at high levels and it is our responsibility to help students reach those levels every day, all day. Next, we will discuss the collaborative nature of special education in chapter 2.

Chapter 1 Reflection

Thinking about the big ideas in chapter 1, such as special education data, *Endrew F.* and *Rowley*, general education first, the inverted triangle, and the wheels of special education, where is your school or district on the stop light?

Red Light Areas Identify practices that must stop	**Yellow Light Areas** Identify essential actions to take	**Green Light Areas** Identify actions to continue

CHAPTER 2
TAKING A COLLABORATIVE APPROACH

If you can't fly, then run.
If you can't run, then walk.
If you can't walk, then crawl.
But by all means, keep moving forward.

—Martin Luther King Jr.

If we were to engage on a journey that is long or difficult, we wouldn't necessarily say, "Well, because it's so far or difficult to get there, we are not going to even attempt to begin." Once we have considered where we are starting from and our goal or endpoint, we create a pathway to get to our goal. If a student requires accommodations to demonstrate their learning or to be able to access the learning environment more successfully, the IEP goals can be aligned to the student's disability and areas of need based on the collected data documenting why the team is recommending the specific accommodation.

Only 54 percent of students identified for special education services graduate with a diploma, according to the National Center for Education Statistics (2020) provided by the U.S. Department of Education. During the 2021–2022 school year, 74 percent of students with IEPs graduated from high school; however, these students had a 17.5 percent lower rate of graduating on time than of individuals who didn't have an IEP. According to the National School Boards Association (2019), roughly two of every three students identified for services graduate with a high school diploma in four years. One out of every three IEP-identified students will take longer than four years to graduate, will graduate with an alternate diploma, or will not graduate at all (table 2.1, page 26).

Table 2.1: Percentage of General Education Participation

Year	80 percent or more of time in general education	40 percent to 79 percent of time in general education	Less than 40 percent of time in general education
2009	59	21	15
2010	61	20	14
2011	61	20	14
2012	61	20	14
2013	62	19	14
2014	62	19	14
2015	63	19	14
2016	63	19	13
2017	63	18	13
2018	64	18	13
2019	65	18	13
2020	66	17	13

Source: National Center for Education Statistics, 2020.

In general education curriculum and instructional planning, educators frequently use the concept of *must know* versus *nice to know* in identifying the standards that carry the greatest leverage for learning. To improve graduation rates of students identified for services and to work meaningfully toward intentional student growth, we propose that special education teams work in collaboration with students' general education teachers to establish goals designed toward meeting the most essential grade-level standards. In *Taking Action*, educators Mike Mattos, Austin Buffum, Janet Malone, Luis F. Cruz, Nicole Dimich, and Sarah Schuhl (2025) share why it is vital for instruction for students to be on grade level. When students are sorted into tracks based on perceived ability and prior success, they are placed according to those with greater academic potential being in higher tracks and those with perceived lower potential being on lower tracks, leading to lower gains. If a student is taken out of a grade-level curriculum and placed in a remedial class, then the student is taught below grade level. Where will this student be by the end of another year? The answer is that the student will remain below grade level. Author Ken Williams (2022) shares in *Ruthless Equity* that "students in low-ability groups are considered inferior and thus unworthy of your most engaging, collaborative, creative, and innovative teaching strategies. Instead, they are relegated to your 'basement best,' a diminished, dumbed-down version of you" (p. 103). While we know there is no universal one-size-fits-all approach, what we also know from John Hattie's (2011) research on meta-analysis is that tracking student learning has only a 0.12 standard deviation and a negative effect on student learning, whereas collective teacher efficacy and teams' belief that they can positively impact students has an effect size of 1.57, the highest effect size of the 150 strategies explored through the study. When the Council for Exceptional Children (2024) identified the practices within the field of special education that carried the most leverage for student learning, it identified three subcategories under collaboration that held the most impact: (1) collaborate with professionals to increase student success, (2) organize and facilitate effective meetings with professionals and families, and (3) collaborate with families to support student learning and secure needed services. When we work together as high-functioning teams, regardless of our support for general education core curriculum or specially designed instruction and intervention, we have the power and ability to improve student outcomes. Each day that we improve student outcomes, we are improving student learning and building a stronger bridge toward graduation and post-secondary life success for all students. We also advocate for teams to craft IEP goals aligned to the *most critical* areas students must know and avoid the *nice-to-know* areas, aligning with the beliefs that holding students and ourselves accountable for high levels of essential learning is the path toward adult independence and success. This chapter discusses understanding what are essential versus nice-to-know standards, identifying priority standards, and aligning IEP goals.

Understanding Essential Versus Nice-to-Know Standards

When teams are deciding what are essential or must-know standards, they discuss what the standards mean and how much time to devote toward mastery. This same level of focus and intentional planning toward mastery is vital when determining IEP goals. Teams must ensure the skills they identify in their goals are the most essential and carry the greatest leverage, depth, and generalization for students to be successful within the education environment. We could spend hours or days working on fact fluency for a student in middle school, or we could teach them how to use a calculator to complete the computation. A *must-know* is how to solve a multistep equation. A *nice-to-know* standard is mathematics fluency facts in middle school. Is there a time and place to teach mathematics fluency? Absolutely! For a student in middle school, is that the most important skill to focus on? The answer is maybe not. Another example of written expression is teaching the five-sentence paragraph. It's important. However, is that the most important piece of written expression? It isn't always.

When teams come together to determine the skills to focus on for a student's IEP, it is essential to start by examining the grade-level expected priority standards and then create goals that demonstrate the specially designed instruction the teams will provide to the student to reach those goals. Functionally, we want to have students demonstrate age-appropriate skills that are essential for lifelong success. When teams start to address a student's executive functioning skills or functional behavior skills, they have to consider what is the largest area that is impacting a student's ability to make progress without support. Providing specially designed instruction to meet the student's impact area and providing strategies or techniques the student can implement within the classroom allow them greater access to the learning environment.

Identifying Priority Standards

Because many general education teams are familiar with building and working through a guaranteed and viable curriculum, selected power or essential standards, and using these to anchor their instruction, they can readily identify a nice-to-know versus a need-to-know standard. Mattos and colleagues (2025) share that a learning-focused school needs to ensure that all students learn at high levels, clarifying that high levels are grade level or better. Therefore, grade-level teams come together to identify the most essential standards that students must learn versus covering every single standard. Developing a guaranteed and viable curriculum focused on student learning means that all students can learn the critical content of the curriculum and that teachers know what is designated as essential (Eaker & Marzano, 2020). While all standards are important and none should be ignored, we also know that some standards hold more leverage, have greater endurance, and have more relevance. When we have identified priority standards and ensured that we are focusing on what students must learn rather than what we will teach, we focus on these areas to identify essential learning outcomes and a core instructional framework. District and school teams that have engaged in the process of identifying priority standards have completed a process of unpacking the standards and determining which standards have the most focus areas in the unit planning as part of their guaranteed and viable curriculum. For more information on how to identify priority standards and standards unpacking, you can use the second edition of *Common Formative Assessment: A Toolkit for Professional Learning Communities at Work* (Bailey & Jakicic, 2023) or *Collaborative Common Assessments* (Erkens, 2016).

General education teams start by determining the standards that provide a student with opportunities to demonstrate their knowledge and skills in multiple areas. Next, they consider the specific endurance of a standard by looking at its focus on knowledge and skills beyond a specific unit or date. Finally, they look at readiness, which are standards that allow for the knowledge and skills necessary for future grades.

In practice, this standards assessment process ensures that general education teachers spend the largest amount of their instructional time devoted to areas students *must* know. Yet, if you were to ask special education teachers across the United States how they determine essential learning standards for the students on their caseload, you might not get the same degree of focus on their responses. When special education teachers engage in forward planning for a student's IEP goals, sometimes a single individual is creating what they think is best, next, or possible. This can lead to a student's instructional plan being created and delivered based on the knowledge and skill of only one person. If you were to ask if a special education teacher spends time collaborating with their counterparts on building a goal that focuses on the priority standards aligned to the student's disability, what kind of responses do you think you would receive? Would you hear conversations or review meeting notes about the student's current levels of performance and the instructional plan to be delivered? When grade-level teams are discussing the priority standards and designing their unit plans, is the special education teacher part of those conversations? Does everyone have regular access to planning documents to inform their instruction?

When the special education teacher is involved in these conversations, it allows them to know what the priority grade-level standards are and to consider how to craft the goal. Their target is to close the learning gap in a way that is aligned with the grade-level standards. Collaborative teams, who want to be intentional for student learning, analyze the goal from multiple viewpoints to find the most ambitious area to focus their efforts. Are they spending their time working on what has the most leverage, endurance, and readiness for this student to close the gap and make progress within the general education environment?

We believe that all students are capable of making high levels of growth and learning. However, growth looks different based on the individual student. Based on *Taking Action* (Mattos et al., 2025) and *Yes We Can!* (Friziellie, Schmidt, & Spiller, 2016), the question that we pose to our teams is, Will the student ever be expected to function independently?

When the answer is yes, the team believes the student is expected to function independently in life as an adult, then the student is capable of high levels of growth and learning, and the expectation for grade-level mastery remains consistent. When a student is expected to be fully independent in life post–high school or as an adult, the team must take every step to ensure it is closing any learning gaps and providing grade-level standards as part of the understanding of content mastery. By writing rigorous IEP goals, the team will continue to close the gap for the student, and the student will be able to demonstrate grade-level content knowledge, even if the student may not be currently performing at grade level or be multiple grade levels below.

If our goal is independence as an adult, when providing accommodations, we need, when possible, a plan to fade the accommodations. If a team recommends, as a result of data collection and problem solving, that a student needs to have their tests read aloud or take the test in a smaller setting, how can the student be supported? What learning strategies could be used to no longer require these accommodations? A better approach might be to create a plan for how the student can be supported within the general education setting and be able to access the material and demonstrate their knowledge through strategies and skills rather than removing the barrier as the first approach. Some students will need supports to allow them to demonstrate their knowledge; however, included with those supports also should be intentional plans to support the student in a variety of settings. In chapter 7 (page 85), we go into detail on how teams can determine supporting accommodations for students.

What if the student is not expected to function independently? Once a team has established beyond a doubt that a student is not expected to function independently in adult life, the teams need to evaluate the profile of the student and discuss the greatest areas of strength and the concerns or impact of the disability (figure 2.1).

Will This Student Be Expected to Function Independently?	
YES	**NO**
Critical Mindset	**Critical Mindset**
Students are capable of high levels (grade-level or higher) of growth and learning.	Students are capable of high levels of growth and learning.
Critical Actions	**Critical Actions**
Every effort is made to ensure students learn grade-level expectations.	Every effort is made to ensure students learn grade-level expectations.
Accommodations aligned to IEP goals are provided.	Accommodations and modifications aligned to IEP goals are provided.
Standards are not modified.	Standards *may* be modified. Use caution when doing this.

Source: *Adapted from Friziellie et al., 2016.*

Figure 2.1: Will this student be expected to function independently?

Once the team identifies areas for growth that will have the most impact on generalization or success, the team can then begin the process of personalizing the standards and, when necessary, modifying the outcomes. Most importantly, this is a *team*-based decision and must include the students' families' viewpoints. Teams must continue to expect every student to continually demonstrate growth even after modifying the standard; however, this growth will be individualized for the student.

Aligning for Alternative Assessments

We can accomplish this by aligning our IEP goal instruction to the grade-level alternative standards, state-approved alternative assessments, or *Dynamic Learning Maps*, which are the alternate assessments that many states use to monitor student growth (sometimes known as essential elements). A student's goals are intentionally designed toward specific targets for learning with growth expected. If the student has some higher-level skills in certain areas, teams can design a combination of grade-level and modified-grade-level expectations that build on student strengths while addressing the areas of need. Within special education, we have to acknowledge the black and white of the law and school code, but also the gray area of understanding how to implement the best instructional plan for the student.

Conclusion

When we hold ourselves to the expectation of intentional collaborative planning so that all students can learn at high levels, we elevate the learning environment to a place where learning is required and not by invitation. This expectation that learning is required also applies to students entitled to receive services. The intentional collaborative efforts between the general education teacher, teams, and special education teacher are essential to building the expectation of high levels of learning for *all* students. Our goal within special education is to increase a student's abilities to learn on their own and to demonstrate their skills throughout the school day. In chapter 3, we explore the partnership between families and the school team as families are also essential members of the student's IEP team.

Chapter 2 Reflection

Based on table 2.1 (page 26), what do the data and essential standards for your district or school look like? Are you answering the question from figure 2.1 regularly? Where is your school or district on the red light for these ideas?

Red Light Areas	**Yellow Light Areas**	**Green Light Areas**
Identify practices that must stop	Identify essential actions to take	Identify actions to continue

CHAPTER 3
INCLUDING PARENTS AND GUARDIANS AS PARTNERS IN THE IEP PROCESS

Accessibility is being able to get in the building.
Diversity is getting invited to the table.
Inclusion is having a voice at the table.
Belonging is having your voice heard at the table.

—The Council for Persons with Disabilities

For many parents, guardians, and families, the IEP journey is something they are incredibly unfamiliar with, especially when a student first becomes eligible for services. Parents, guardians, and families may be unsure or unaware of all of the necessary steps the IEP process includes and may not realize how vital of a role parents and guardians are to the team. With IDEA (2004) and its subsequent reauthorizations, the role of families as partners in the IEP process has been continually reaffirmed and included. The rights of parents and guardians under IDEA include being present at meetings for their child but having information be meaningful to allow them to make informed decisions regarding their child. Parents, guardians, and families may have previous experiences with the public school system that can impact their ability to engage in the IEP planning process. Their engagement can also be dependent on the individual family's culture and beliefs toward public schooling. The role of the school team is to ensure students are educated and also provide continuous information to families to help them be meaningful participants in the IEP process. While some families may not need any additional information, or they have plenty of resources for outside advice on the planning process, school teams still have a responsibility to ensure that they are partnering with the family in planning for the student.

School teams embrace the power of collaboration and collaborative structures to set the foundation for success, which is vital to the success of students receiving services. Students are dependent on school teams' abilities to provide exceptional learning experiences and function as high-performing collaborative teams across all stakeholders, within the school buildings, and outside of our schools. Instead of creating a divide between the home providers and a school team, it is essential to work together to use collective responsibility for students to overcome any barriers that are preventing them from making progress. In some cases, families have private providers, therapists, and support members who contribute to a student's success. When we work together to collaborate and share strategies, ideas, and goals between the school and home, we can build more powerful connections. Teams need to focus all their efforts on the *right* work. When teams agree on the *right* work, they know that what they are doing and spending their time focusing on is creating higher levels of learning for students and is designed to meet their individual needs.

There is no shortage of memes and cartoons that document parental and school team feelings toward attending IEP meetings for their children. As collaborative educators, it is our deepest desire to have teams break down these myths and approach IEP meetings as an opportunity for everyone involved to come together to not only celebrate strengths but also build the plan for the individual student's future. These meetings are a time to dream big. Although these dreams may seem scary, they will create a roadmap for learning for the student. Time after time, we see where students can reach a new level of learning or opportunity after a team has built scaffolds and strategies for the student to demonstrate their learning. Teams build upon their knowledge and experiences, and each time a barrier is broken for a student, it only creates more opportunities for the student to have additional adventures in the future. The team's job is to create as many adventure pathways as possible to allow the student and their family to have options as the student grows. These pathways start with collaborative relationships across the entire team where they are all fundamentally committed to one thing: the student's growth.

We want teams to understand that when they embrace the requirements set forth by IDEA (2004), they are building a partnership that is in the best interest of the student. When parents and guardians and private teams are viewed with a sense of partnership and belonging at the IEP table, the team has done their job successfully. It is their responsibility, after ensuring appropriate instruction and ambitious plans for the students, to continually build on partnerships with families. There is no greater trust than the trust that families give each day when they send their students into our care. This trust is magnified greatly when the student has specialized learning needs and requires more than the core curriculum to make progress. Further, it is magnified tenfold when the student has extensive needs, such as being unable to communicate or move independently, or has complex learning needs. In these scenarios, the degree of collaboration and partnership between home and school plays a vital role in the success of not only the student but the entire team.

IDEA includes that the opportunity for parent participation in the IEP is required (Cornell Law School,, n.d.), but sometimes school district teams are not sure what such participation means or looks like. Some schools think inviting parents and guardians to the meetings is parent participation, others might ask parents and guardians how they think things are going in participation, but in reality, neither of those things are enough. Parents and guardians deserve to be equal participants in the development of their student's IEP. IDEA states that "Each public agency must take steps to ensure that one or both of the parents [and guardians] of a child with a disability are present at each IEP Team meeting or are afforded the opportunity to participate" (Cornell Law School, n.d.). The expectations included in IDEA (2004) assist school district teams in tasks that need to be done to meet the requirements of the law. We break down these steps in this chapter to focus on the different ways in which teams have met the IDEA guidelines to ensure we are scheduling the IEP meeting, making parent participation at the meeting meaningful, using PATH and MAPS for person-centered planning, getting input from private providers, and timing the drafting of the proposed IEP.

Scheduling the IEP Meeting

First, the school team must work with the parents and guardians to schedule a meeting and agree on a time and place. Often, school teams believe the IEP meeting must take place at school, but other locations, such as a library, are permissible under the law. Sometimes, school teams struggle with scheduling a meeting as parents' and guardians' work schedules and the school teams' schedules are not always compatible. We always encourage both the parents and guardians and the school team to be creative when scheduling the meeting, so that it works for both parties. It is vital for schools to reach out to parents and guardians and provide options, when possible for the meeting, including the day, time, and method.

Since the COVID-19 pandemic, school teams have become more flexible by offering virtual meetings for families to participate via platforms such as Zoom (https://zoom.us) or Google Meet (https://meet.google.com). It is also important for school teams to be flexible with the day and time for the meeting. If our goal is to truly have parents and guardians as partners, we will reach out to parents and guardians with options for the meeting that reflect both the school day and the parents' or guardians' availability. This can be a shift for some schools where an IEP Day is designated, which is the only day meetings can be scheduled. Therefore, if a parent or guardian works on Tuesdays, which is the designated meeting day, can the team be flexible and schedule the meeting for another day? One district we worked with set all of the meetings on a calendar in August and simply emailed the parents a notification telling them the date and time. While advance notice can be helpful and ensure the meetings are all scheduled, is this creating an inviting atmosphere for families when one-half of the team arbitrarily determines the day and time of the meeting without even asking if that date was available for the other half? If a family emailed the school and stated there would be a meeting on a specific day and time without requesting availability, most schools would have difficulty with ensuring coverage and availability. So, parents or guardians need to be offered the same considerations as the school team. School teams can reach out to parents and guardians through a variety of methods such as calling or emailing to request parents' and guardians' availability within a two- or three-week period or sending preselected time slots through a software program, or even in an email to allow the parent to select the one that would best fit or propose other options.

Once the meeting is scheduled, the school district is required to send notice of the time, location, purpose of the meeting, and who from the school team will be present at the meeting and has knowledge of the student or expertise that can contribute to the discussion about the student in accordance with IDEA (Cornell Law School, 2007). If a parent is unavailable after multiple tries to attend an IEP meeting, the school team should document the attempts to get the parent to attend. The team should continue their open communication with the family and share what was discussed at the IEP meeting. It should be a rare occasion that parents or guardians do not attend the IEP meeting if the school is being creative and thinking outside the box about helping the parents or guardians to attend the meeting.

Making Participation Meaningful

Since parent, guardian, and even student participation, when appropriate, is needed in the process, school teams must ensure that they have full and meaningful participation and are equal members of the IEP team so that they are engaged in the process and are valuable members of the team. This can be done in several ways.

Teams have many options for encouraging and gaining meaningful participation from families. Beginning with the start of the school year, individualized communications build rapport and establish connections. Continual updates and seeking input from families throughout the year regarding their perspectives and thoughts on upcoming goals and needs for the IEP are also beneficial.

District leaders have a responsibility to ensure that special education staff are aware of district procedures and expectations when partnering with parents and guardians. If there are no expectations yet, leadership must use this as an opportunity to build expectations with the teams. They also need to create that understanding with families that their goal is to partner together to build the IEP collaboratively, and input is not only allowed but sought after and valued. A quote shared by the Council for Persons with Disabilities (2021) states, "Accessibility is being able to get in the building. Diversity is getting invited to the table. Inclusion is having a voice at the table. Belonging is having your voice heard at the table." While the quote is geared toward ensuring individuals with disabilities are more than simply included, it is also the same for families to experience true belonging at the IEP table and with the school team.

Prior to each IEP meeting, one IDEA requirement is for school teams to collaborate with the parents and guardians and family team so that the family can have meaningful input on the creation of the IEP. To ensure parents and guardians are engaged in the process of participation, they can share their input on the student's strengths, weaknesses, and any concerns ahead of the meeting as well as during the meeting. Meaningful parent input is more than just asking, "How do you think things have been going this year?" One option is to have parents and guardians fill out a structured family input form to engage them in a discussion about the student's strengths, areas for improvement, goals for the future, and other items that the parents and guardians feel are important. See the reproducible "Family IEP Input" (page 42) to help with getting meaningful family input.

Using PATH and MAPS for Person-Centered Planning

School teams and families should engage at the beginning of the school year so that school teams can obtain an understanding of the parents' and guardians' hopes, dreams, and wishes for their child's future as well as to begin to build the relationship for the rest of the school year. Schools can engage in person-centered planning as a tool to build a shared understanding of the student's future. In these conversation-based planning structures, the family, school, and any other key stakeholders, such as outside therapy teams, come together to imagine the future for the student and to map how to reach these goals.

One part of person-centered planning focuses on the Planning for Alternative Tomorrows with Hope (PATH) and Making Action Plans (MAPS) processes explained in *The PATH and MAPS Handbook* (O'Brien, Pearpoint, & Kahn, 2015). In the PATH format, the team centers the conversation around the student's future goal and builds specific actions that must be taken through a timeline, building the student's roadmap to their goal by committing specific people, timelines, and action steps for the team members. For this process to be successful, the teams must have open and honest dialogue around what the student's current structures look like as well as the timeline for the future and action steps. In some cases, it can be easier for teams to feel that they are protecting the parent if they don't fully explain what the student's day looks like at school. However, families must have a full understanding of the level of support required for their students and what they are working on at school to build a solid understanding of the student's skills.

Using PATH

When school teams engage in a person-centered planning approach using the PATH process, it includes a holistic approach to the whole student. This approach includes support for the student from both home and school, working in collaboration with one another toward mutual outcomes that look ahead with parents and guardians, to plan how each school year or IEP year is part of the student's long-term future.

Using MAPS

In the MAPS planning process, the team begins with the history of the student. Using a MAPS planning process, the team identifies the student's story, including past and present experiences; identifies key individuals in the student's life; and recognizes action steps, student needs, student gifts, and strengths. One of the key concepts of MAPS is to build a meaningful relationship with the family, hear their dreams, recognize what may be scary, and build a shared picture of the daily actions that contribute to the dreams. Then, the team uses structured questions to help the family and team share different key pieces of information or highlight the milestones they have reached. They try to build a deeper connection and dream together so that they can then build a plan in the direction of those dreams.

While each family has different expectations of the school teams, you can't ever assume that you know everything about a student from their paperwork. Engaging in a collaborative conversation regarding the student's progress and the family's current goals allows the school team and the family to connect as early as possible to begin the year's collaborative structures. This should be more than simply sharing contact information and an introductory email. School teams who make the time to ensure they are setting the foundation early in the school year are better prepared to have difficult conversations later if the need arises. The family knows the team is invested in their child because they have been in communication since the beginning of the school year and have had open conversations about wanting to get to know the student and the family from a partnership approach.

Getting Input From Private Providers

Another part of the process of getting input is when students have a private provider; we need to ensure we are getting input from those who work with the student or family. Some families opt to have school-based therapies as well as private therapy to support the student in areas the school does not focus on or in addition to the work taking place within the school. If you have students who have these services outside of school, we encourage you to have the families sign releases to allow you to speak to the private providers about services. The release allows you, the private providers, or the school-based clinician to have an open discussion about what everyone is seeing in terms of the student's work. To foster shared growth and begin collaboration, it is important to communicate early with the private provider. While, at times, school-based staff are not able to mimic private therapy and vice versa, it does not mean we can't all partner and update each other on progress and strategies being implemented. School-based and clinic-based providers both develop areas of need, but these areas could be different due to the requirements of IDEA in schools and insurance needs for the clinic. For example, a clinic-based physical therapist may work on skills such as range of motion, stability, and strengthening, whereas a school-based physical therapist focuses on safely navigating the school environment. Having this information as part of the IEP process is essential and allows the providers who work with the family and student to have input. When teams engage in collaboration between school and private therapy, many different avenues can be opened, including for related service staff to have a thought partner or problem-solving partner when working on strategies, especially if the school or district does not have larger related service teams for job-alike partners to come together often. The reproducible "Private Provider Planning Collaboration Tool" (page 44) can help teams work with private providers.

Timing the Drafting of the Proposed IEP

In many states, such as Illinois, there are requirements for how early a team has to produce a draft copy of certain pieces of the proposed IEP prior to the meeting. In Illinois, Article 14 of the School Code (Illinois State Board of Education, 2020) states that all public schools must provide "copies of all the written materials" (p. 37) that will be considered in the IEP meeting at a minimum of three school days before the meeting. The written materials include the following.

- Evaluation materials
- Collected data
- IEP components
- Present levels
- Closed goals
- Draft proposed goals
- Draft proposed accommodations

This can be a large area of frustration for teams that haven't fully understood the purpose behind these requirements. When teams view preparing documents and sharing them with families as an additional task they have to do or one that opens them up to scrutiny from the family, it misses the spirit of what IDEA requires for meaningful parental participation. Having the draft documents in advance allows parents and guardians to come to the meeting with a full understanding of what the team will be proposing and be able to have time to digest this information, form any necessary questions, and use the vital meeting time as an opportunity for open dialogue between everyone to plan for the upcoming year. Ideally, we want to ensure parents and guardians have enough time to review the documents, ask questions, and consider their viewpoints on what they see as best for their student. This can be met in a variety of formats, with some teams reaching out as early as a month prior to the meeting to begin the dialogue and gather input. Finally, as part of the PLAAFP, there is a specific section that is titled "Parent Concerns" or "Parent Input" within the IEP. The section is specifically designed and included to ensure the parent, guardian, or family input is included and considered throughout the IEP. Parents' and guardians' input needs to address any negative concerns and also gain their input and desires for the student for the upcoming year. Oftentimes, these can be perceived as "concerns" in a negative mindset; however, when approached from a lens of collaboration and building the best plan for the student, this section of the IEP can be framed as parent or guardian input into the plan. Likewise, this section can be modified throughout the meeting to build on a parent's or guardian's participation.

Conclusion

In chapter 4, we will begin the process of creating the IEP that will guide the team for the year. One of the most critical but often overlooked components of the IEP is the present levels of academic achievement and functional performance. This section of the IEP more commonly known as the present levels gives the team a foundation for the goals and current levels for the student. If it were a book, it would be the introduction compiled with many data points to accurately articulate to the reader why the book is being written. Throughout our experiences, a strong and well-written present levels page has served as a source of documentation, and a starting point for the IEP.

Chapter 3 Reflection

When it comes to the student's IEP, does the parent or guardian have a sense of belonging as part of the IEP team? What steps does the team initiate to support parental or guardian collaboration?

Red Light Areas	**Yellow Light Areas**	**Green Light Areas**
Identify practices that must stop	Identify essential actions to take	Identify actions to continue

Family IEP Input

Hello! We are looking forward to the upcoming IEP meeting for _____ on _____. As _____'s family we want to ensure your input is part of the IEP process. To help the team begin to prepare for the meeting, we are seeking your feedback below. If you can, please return the completed form to _____ by _____ so that we have time to prepare for the meeting.

Name of person completing: _____

Date: _____

What are your student's strengths at school and at home?

What are your student's biggest challenges at school and at home?

Thinking forward to the next year, what are the immediate goals you have for _____?

Thinking forward to the next five years, what are the goals you have for _____?

If you feel comfortable sharing, in relation to _____'s education, what are your fears for this upcoming year1

page 1 of 2

The Collaborative IEP © 2025 Solution Tree Press • SolutionTree.com
Visit **go.SolutionTree.com/specialneeds** to download this free reproducible.

What are the most important areas you focus on at home?

What does independence look like for your student?

What is the most important area for your student to have success?

What would a successful year look like for _____?

Are there any specific areas that you want to discuss or concerns you have for _____'s plan?

Private Provider Planning Collaboration Tool

_____'s strengths in private therapy include:

_____'s areas for growth in private therapy include:

Thinking forward to the next year, what are the immediate goals you have for _____?

What areas do you see overlapping with the areas focused on at school?

Are there any specific strategies or tools that have been helpful in private therapy?

Are there any specific strategies or tools that have not been successful in private therapy?

PART 2

The How

CHAPTER 4
WRITING THE PLAAFP STATEMENT

Knowledge is only the first step. It is the foundation of further learning processes.

—Inez De Florio

For a student identified to receive special education services, the IEP serves as the vehicle that drives the student's educational journey. With each section of information, beginning with the PLAAFP and the goals, accommodations, service minutes, and placement through the designated progress monitoring, the IEP changes course based on the information provided over time. Just as the car responds to the speed, road conditions, and directions, we too respond to how a student is learning through the information and data obtained each day. For a car to move forward effectively, all components must be in place, support one another, and work together to allow the car to run smoothly.

The PLAAFP statements within an IEP are the foundational structure on which the proposed new IEP rests. The remainder of the IEP should be tied directly back to the data and information from the PLAAFP; the need for the specific goals and accommodations are documented in a well-written PLAAFP. From a collaborative team structure, the PLAAFP is one of the key areas in which the general education team has as much, if not more, information to add to the IEP. A well-written PLAAFP provides information for the team to have a clear understanding of the student's academic strengths, functional performance, and current challenges for the school year. A brief update about the student's goals and plans for achieving these goals is included in the PLAAFP. In some ways, if you think of the IEP as a book, then the PLAAFP is chapter 1, providing data and details to let you know what the book is about and what to expect. In this chapter, we break down the PLAAFP, paragraph by paragraph, including academic achievement, functional performance, and any related service areas such as communication, motor function, or social-emotional needs to help teams be diligent in crafting an exceptional PLAAFP to provide the layers necessary for a strong IEP.

Components of the PLAAFP

Each state and district may have its own requirements for PLAAFP completion, which must always be considered locally; however, meeting those requirements does not necessarily mean that the team has a well-constructed PLAAFP. Some states may require the PLAAFP to include goal updates, independence, social-emotional levels, and vocational levels, even if the student is not receiving services in those areas, regardless of any specific state requirements. A well-crafted PLAAFP should always include the following areas.

- Parent educational concerns and input
- Present levels of student's academic performance (both strength areas and areas that need improvement)
- Present levels of student's functional and developmental performance (both strength areas and areas that need improvement)
- Most recent evaluation results (may be a state-by-state requirement; if not required as a separate section, the data should be included under academic or functional performance)
- The impact statement or effect of the student's disability (including how the disability is impacting the student's progress within the general education setting)

Although the team drives the IEP creation process, the general education teacher plays a larger role in preparing the PLAAFP statement for the IEP. The general education teacher supports the student's learning, and their input is vital for a well-rounded, data-driven statement that includes details on how the student is performing in comparison to grade-level peers.

Starting With Strengths

When discussing a student's progress, many times we can spend the entirety of a meeting focusing on the areas in which a student is not making expected progress or is discrepant from their same-grade peers. From a planning perspective, this can make planning based on a strengths-based model very difficult if the focus is mainly on the negative pieces. As a collaborative team, you want to ensure you are all focusing on the areas in which a student can and does perform and use those strengths for future planning. In some states, a separate section of the IEP titled "Student Strengths" begins the PLAAFP; in others, it begins with academics and functional performance. Regardless of the state requirements, the collaborative team must always maintain a focus on the strengths the student brings to school each day as well as the individual needs the student has that require specially designed instruction.

When discussing student strengths, PLAAFP statements should include information from a variety of staff members, the classroom teacher, the special area teachers, interventionists, and the members of the special education team for both academic and functional skills. The PLAAFP is a prime opportunity to demonstrate how well the team knows *how* the student learns. Avoid open storytelling such as, "Last week, when we were working on a math problem, Allie solved it all by herself." While telling these stories is well-intentioned, the purpose of the PLAAFP is to share data and information about what the student can and cannot do within the classroom setting. Therefore, it is essential to discuss *actual* student strengths in *how* they learn at school. Teams need to be specific and data-driven in their statements by utilizing sentences such as, "Cindy can solve two-digit by two-digit addition and subtraction problems independently. However, she requires visuals and support to solve two-digit by two-digit multiplication problems, whereas same-aged peers are able to solve three-digit by three-digit addition, subtraction, multiplication, and division problems independently." See figure 4.1 for examples of how to write strengths statements for a PLAAFP.

Weak Statements	Strong Statements
Vague statements such as the following. • He's a sweet boy and a kind friend. • She's very sociable and likes to be with peers. • Tommy always makes me smile. • He's a good listener. • She tries very hard.	• Tenley can decode grade-level text. • Julie solves mathematics word problems that include only addition independently. • Tommy has built strong relationships with peers in the class and is the first to volunteer to help a peer.
Open-ended stories such as the following. • Last week, when we were working on our math problems, Alice solved it all by herself. • At recess, John really enjoys playing and has been playing the team games.	• Alice has been demonstrating more independence in completing her math word problems before asking for help. • John has recently been initiating group games at recess or asking to join other games if they are already in progress.

Figure 4.1: Examples of strong and weak strengths statements for a PLAAFP.

Often, after an IEP meeting, when reflecting on what went well or could have been improved, the team (general education teacher, special education teacher, and related services) can consider if the information shared demonstrated a strength or was something that should have been told to the parent before the IEP meeting. For example, when the student did something for the first time or had a learning breakthrough, the team should share that by emailing the parent when it happened.

Ongoing communication throughout the year is one of the most essential tasks a school team can do to update families about how the student is growing in their skills. Therefore, don't wait until an IEP meeting to share information with the family. The IEP meeting is only one of the times we communicate in person with a family. Therefore, the IEP meeting serves as a formality, with the majority of the information already known to the family. No one likes surprises at IEP meetings.

One way to ensure that the team has considered strengths and challenges across the student's educational day is to use a consistent structure to gather feedback from all the educators working with a student. This can be done in a variety of ways, such as in person, by email, or using a structured form (see the reproducible "Teacher PLAAFP Input Document" on page 56). When general education teachers give input, it's important to have consistency in providing the input in areas such as (see the reproducible for more examples):

- Student progress in coursework
- Student independence
- Student executive functioning skills (turn in work on time, start work, complete work, and so on)
- Questions specifically related to how the disability impacts the student

As a student progresses through grade levels and moves from one classroom teacher during the day to six or seven teachers, it is essential to ensure that the IEP team has an accurate picture of what the student's day looks like, how the student accesses support, as well as their strengths and challenges in different educational environments. The IEP team should also be made aware of how a student is engaging in nonacademic settings.

One section of the PLAAFP is the section on parent concerns for the IEP meeting. IDEA section 300.324 (U.S. Department of Education, 2017d) specifically states that in the creation of an IEP, the IEP team must consider the "concerns of the parents [and guardians] for enhancing the education of their child." School teams need to be open to hearing parents' and guardians' concerns if they intend to become a collaborative team. There are some strategic steps both families and school teams can engage in to use this opportunity to share and have an open dialogue of conversation regarding the student's current and upcoming strengths, challenges, and skills.

To ensure that the IEP meeting is as successful as possible, school teams can and should reach out to families before the meeting to see if they have any concerns as well as gather their input for the meeting (see chapter 3, page 33). This can be accomplished by the special education teacher or case manager and general education teacher setting up a phone call or emailing a structured survey to the family. When a family's concerns are known, the team can prepare answers and possible solutions in time for the meeting. If the team is proactive in gathering the family's input before the meeting, it can foster a successful partnership with the family. Whether the team uses an in-person meeting, virtual meeting, or a phone call to gather this information, it is essential that the school team follow a consistent structure to keep the call focused on the upcoming meeting and gather much-needed input to prepare the draft IEP. To help gather the input from the family, use the reproducible "Family IEP Input" (page 42 in chapter 3).

Academic Achievement

In reporting the academic achievement of the student on the PLAAFP, the team must report across the student's grade-level academic areas. This section needs to include areas of challenge and areas of strength. It is imperative that school teams include this information in family-friendly language so that anyone who reads the document has a clear understanding of how the student is performing academically. Team-created, well-written statements demonstrate the student's current academic performance on district assessments, classroom-based assessments, and goal work (if applicable). At each IEP meeting, the team continually updates the student's progress on the PLAAFP. Academic achievement should include the individual areas of reading, writing, and mathematics. The more details provided by the team to demonstrate the student's current levels, the better. These details demonstrate the specific skill strengths of the student as well as the areas the student has not yet met. An example of a PLAAFP could look like the following.

> ***Strengths (brief example):***
>
> *Riley has really grown this year in her math fact skills. She knows her math facts 0–8 and is one of the most consistent in the class for reaching 100 percent. Riley also has a personal strength in retelling stories after hearing a passage.*
>
> ***Academic Performance (brief example):***
>
> *In reading, Riley has achieved the following scores on her most recent common formative assessments (CFAs):*
>
> *Unit 3 (reading comprehension about the text): 4/5*
>
> *Unit 4 (reading comprehension beyond the text): 1/5*
>
> *On Fall MAP: 145/32nd percentile, meaning she scored at or better than 32 percent of same-grade students who took the test.*
>
> *On Winter MAP: 148/22nd percentile, meaning she scored at or better than 22 percent of same-grade students who took the test.*
>
> *On classroom work, Riley is able to decode a grade-level passage and self-correct when she makes an error in the passage. Riley reads through a*

grade-level passage independently and will look at the pictures while reading. After completing the reading, Riley is able to answer basic questions about the passage, such as who the main character is or where the story takes place. Riley has grown in her ability to retell a story and uses a "first, next, then" visual to help her retell the story accurately. Riley is not yet able to retell a story without visuals or support. Riley needs assistance to return to the text to find an answer to a comprehension question when she does not immediately know the answer. She will guess or make up an answer that she would like to have in the story. By the end of second grade, students should be able to return to a passage to answer comprehension questions and find an answer.

Functional Performance

Functional performance can be more difficult to articulate with data than academic performance. Well-crafted functional performance levels cover a variety of skill areas: classroom routines, work habits, levels of independence, following directions, completing and submitting work, attending and focusing during instruction, and adaptive skills. Accurately documenting these skill areas can be imperative to teams in their planning during the current year as well as for the future.

Classroom routines highlight the student's ability to follow basic classroom expectations such as lining up, turning in assignments, transitioning between locations within the classroom, and following teacher expectations. These can be critical to gather input from special area teachers, such as art, physical education, STEAM, and music, as these are often classes students may not participate in each day or have multiple opportunities in the week to practice the skill. Some of these special area classes may be beneficial areas for student growth that the team should consider when determining the types of environments in which a student is most successful and how support is best provided to create opportunities for success. For example, a student may be able to follow two-step directions in the classroom based on academic skills. However, the student may not be able to follow a two-step direction in physical education class that involves motor control and different physical movements or getting their body in the correct position, such as catching a ball at second base and then throwing it to third base.

The concept of a student's work habits can be hard to articulate for some teams. In some schools, report cards include work habits such as the student's ability to come to class prepared, remain organized, have all their materials, take notes, and engage in study. If your school or district does not yet report work habits on a report card, it is still helpful to consider these areas when thinking about a student's special education needs and progress and how these specific areas can impact a student's academic performance. If you are looking to explore this area more, *Redefining Student Accountability: A Proactive Approach to Teaching Behavior Outside the Gradebook* by Tom Schimmer (2023) might be especially useful for working with students with special needs. For example, work habits may be an area in which a student needs more support, and determining ways to address this requires thoughtful collaboration from the student's IEP team.

Regardless of a student's disability, it is essential that the IEP team determine the student's needs through data based on the student's current level in the classroom and also their strengths and challenges. Depending on the support in the classroom, it may be necessary to track work completion, on-task or off-task behavior, materials organization, or even student participation. As teams come together to build the present levels or PLAAFP, consider that for a student who has been receiving accommodations, the team includes updates or narratives in the present levels regarding how often these are used. This would also include any unofficial accommodations or supports a teacher is providing for the student to be successful.

Accurately documenting a student's level of independence in completing both academic and functional routines determines how a student engages in the activities of the school day. In the PLAAFP, school teams must include whether the student needs individual support, such as additional prompts to complete activities, visuals, or breakdowns of multistep directions to be able to complete the tasks independently. This information creates a clear understanding for everyone about the student's required support level and helps them understand when growth has occurred in terms of reducing that support.

Finally, it is also important to share an update on the student's social-emotional present levels in areas, such as handling frustration, being told "No," winning or losing in a game, and peer relationships. In the event these are not an area of concern for the student, the team can include statements about how the student engages with peers and in gameplay. If this is an area the student requires support, the team needs to indicate how the student interacts in these situations, what support is needed, what the support will look like, and how much support is required. For example, if a student needs support to process a perceived negative interaction with a peer, the IEP update would include a statement about utilizing strategies such as retelling the event from both perspectives or problem solving through identifying alternate outcomes and selecting an alternative strategy to try next time. An example of a functional performance statement is the following.

Functional Performance (brief example):

Riley is doing great at starting her work independently. On the last five data collection opportunities, Riley has begun her assignment or task within 20 seconds, which is a decrease from last year at over one minute to begin a task. Riley requires more support in completing her task and staying on task for the duration of the assignment. Riley can engage in sustained work for about three minutes before she begins to shift to a different focus (getting a different book out, leaving her seat, or talking to a peer). When prompted, Riley will return to the task in about 50 percent of opportunities. After taking a timed or structured break (go to get water or timer and brain break for three minutes), Riley will return to task in about 25 percent of opportunities. By the end of second grade, students are able to engage in sustained work for up to twelve to fifteen minutes and complete an activity.

At the end of the PLAAFP, school teams typically have a section for what is commonly known as the impact statement for describing how the student's disability impacts their ability to make progress within the school. In most cases, this statement remains the same throughout the entire eligibility time and only changes after an evaluation or reevaluation is completed. This statement needs to include any areas in which the team has agreed the student requires special education instruction and the specific areas in which they will be supporting the student. While the best teams can craft this broadly enough to be able to support the student in a variety of ways, this statement must be directly linked to the evaluation areas. The team then uses this statement to determine goal areas and accommodations. Impact statements can include bullet points or statements such as the following example.

Cindy's specific learning disability in basic reading skills impacts her ability to decode unfamiliar words without specially designed instruction. Her specific learning disability in math problem-solving skills impacts her ability to solve grade-level mathematics problems. Cindy's other health impairment impacts her ability to maintain focus and concentration for more than twelve minutes at a time.

Conclusion

When teams come together and create a strong PLAAFP statement for a student, it allows for a solid foundation for the remainder of the student's IEP to be built on. Strong PLAAFPs allow teams to demonstrate data-informed knowledge of exactly where a student's current abilities are within the school environment and how the individual strengths and challenges are impacting a student's progress. They demonstrate from a variety of perspectives about the student's specific strengths and specific challenges. Further, a strong PLAAFP demonstrates exactly what skill areas need to be included in the goals and what accommodations or supports may be necessary for the student's current functioning around the request and determines if the support was necessary.

Similarly, for the evaluation cycle, teams determine progression over three-year periods from the specific details provided within a strong PLAAFP. Even when an area isn't a specific area of concern and doesn't require support, it is still important to create a present level that accurately portrays all areas of the student's educational day. Well-written PLAAFPs allow teams to look back and determine when an area became a concern as well as what previous years looked like as to how the student was performing academically and functionally. When we seek feedback from the teams regarding a student's learning across their school day, we share a structured feedback form such as the one in the reproducible "Team Feedback Form" (page 58) to help teachers and staff know what type of information we are seeking and how to share information that is most relevant for the student's learning.

Now that we have a clear understanding of what a student's academic and functional performance looks like throughout their school day, it's time to build the next layer of our IEP—the student's individual goals. Chapter 5 identifies how IEP teams provide specially designed instruction targeting the student's individual goals with an ambitious mindset of closing the student's learning gap and achieving high levels of success.

Chapter 4 Reflection

How does your team gather feedback from all members of the student's team to build the IEP?

Red Light Areas	**Yellow Light Areas**	**Green Light Areas**
Identify practices that must stop	Identify essential actions to take	Identify actions to continue

Teacher PLAAFP Input Document

Hello,

We have an IEP meeting for _____ scheduled on _____.
To help the IEP team craft the best document to support _____, it is essential that we also have your insight. Please complete and return to _____ by _____.

Just a friendly reminder: Please write this with the understanding it will be shared with the student's family. If you have not yet shared this information with the family, please contact _____ so that we can create an opportunity for you to do so.

Your name and class: _____

Student-Specific Strengths

Instructions: Please be specific and include district and classroom data in your statements.

Academic strengths:

_____

_____

_____

Grades: _____

Areas needing support:

Please be specific and include data to support your statements.

Functional Performance

(Functional performance includes work habits, study skills, attendance, organization, and independence.)

Functional strengths:

Areas needing support:

_____
_____
_____

Are there any supports or accommodations you are providing to help the student be successful?

Are there any supports or accommodations currently written in the student's IEP that they do not use in your class?

Are there any additional comments or work samples you want to share?

Team Feedback Form

It is time to begin planning for _____'s upcoming IEP meeting on _____. As a teacher of _____, your input is most valuable to ensure we have a full picture of _____'s school day. *This information will be shared with the team and with the family.* Please reach out to _____ if you have any questions.

The more detailed information you can provide the better.

Student name: _____

Teacher name: _____

_____'s strengths in your setting:

_____'s areas for improvement in your setting:

_____'s recent grades and assessment results:

Accommodations or supports currently used in your setting:

Are there specific academic, social, or functional concerns you have regarding _____'s progress in your setting?

How would you describe _____'s academic skills?

How would you describe _____'s functional skills (work completion, attention to detail, group work, and so on)?

How would you describe _____'s social-emotional skills (coping strategies, handling frustration or disappointment, and self-advocacy)?

Samples of student work:

CHAPTER 5

WRITING GOALS: GETTING STARTED

In special education, there's too much emphasis placed on the deficit and not enough on the strength.

—Temple Grandin

We have finally made it to starting the road trip of collaboratively planning for the student. Up until now, we have been engaging in the essential tasks of planning and preparing for the journey of the student's IEP year. What often occurs with collaborative teams is that they start here with the goals and then backfill all the information to support the goal. In correlation to a road trip, this would be the equivalent to starting the car and having a broad destination in mind without doing any research on the specifics required to successfully arrive at the destination. Often, teams start thinking about the current goals and planning for future goals without taking the time to review current data, consider student strengths, consider what other team members may be working on, or even talk with the family and student when appropriate. For this chapter, we will look at IEP planning through a lens similar to planning a trip, before delving into writing IEP goals, asking two critical questions for the goals, and writing goals as a team.

Kristen's Travel Analogy

When it comes to travel, I'm a planner. Have you ever ventured onto a vacation or road trip to visit somewhere you've been before? Often, we don't plan as much as we do when visiting a new location because we settle into a familiar routine.

When I was growing up, there was a place my family visited each year. As an adult, I found myself wanting to repeat this experience because of my memories of mostly positive experiences around this particular location. When it came time to go with my adult family, I relied on my previous knowledge for our trip. Wow, that was a mistake. Many of the places I had fond childhood memories of had changed or were no longer in business. We spent the first part of each day figuring out options. The upside is that we encountered new activities that we didn't know were options because we didn't do any research before the trip. The lack of planning made the journey more challenging and brought with it anxiety I could have avoided.

Megan's Travel Analogy

Kristen and I travel very differently. She prefers to drive, and I prefer to fly, as driving can be boring. She will listen to a book in the car or a podcast, with some music thrown in occasionally, especially if it's Taylor Swift. I'm different. If I had to drive, I would sing along to 90s music in the hopes of speeding up the drive. Driving, to me, is a waste of valuable time that I could be spending at my destination, especially since I prefer to go to tropical places. My focus is to get to my destination with plenty of time, but I will take risks and be more flexible for a better deal to get home. Being educators, traveling during the breaks is tough as that is when most families travel. From my experience, it is better to have a plan of how you are going to get there, and you can make changes during the vacation, but you are in your favorite location and doing rewarding things.

Writing IEP Goals

Our travel analogies paint the picture of how many educators write IEP goals. In many ways, this is the process that teams embark on when they start thinking about the annual review for the student. IDEA requires that school teams review student progress and determine goals at least annually or within a twelve-month period. This is termed the annual or annual review (U.S. Department of Education, 2017d). As the annual review approaches, the IEP team begins to think about where the student is currently with their skills, what the upcoming year will look like for the student, and ideas for goals to support the student's growth. This can be a challenging process for teams to ensure they are making informed decisions in identifying the most important areas for the student in the next twelve months. At this stage, teams begin the process by looking at the present-level academic and functional data for the student. They consider all the different strengths a student has as well as their challenges based on how their disability impacts them. From there, they begin to plan goals for the student. Teams should consider using a strengths-based planning process (outlined in chapter 4, page 47) to determine future goals. Thinking through a strengths-based planning mindset allows the team to recognize the student's academic and cognitive competence. When IEP teams focus only on the deficits, they miss opportunities to capitalize on a strength area for the student. Therefore, when considering the student's learning needs, the team needs to identify the student's strengths first and how those strengths can help the student in their areas of challenge. As teams craft goals, they focus on the IDEA requirements, which is their legal responsibility. However, the human responsibility is to maximize every growth area for the student and capitalize on their strengths to ensure that every student is held to the highest expectations possible.

For teams that are part of school- or districtwide learning communities, there is an expectation of maintaining high levels of learning for all students. PLCs at Work, for example, focus on four critical questions to guarantee student learning: (1) What do we want students to know and be able to do? (2) How will we know if they learned it? (3) What will we do to support students who haven't learned it yet? and (4) How will we extend learning for students who have learned it? (DuFour, DuFour, Eaker, Many, Mattos, & Muhammad, 2024). Regardless of the organizing principles of a school's or district's teams, they are always working to the grade-level standard or the individualized alternative grade-level standard (for when the student is not expected to function independently in life).

In *Yes We Can!*, authors Heather Friziellie, Julie Schmidt, and Jeanne Spiller (2016) share the importance of teaching to the grade-level standard and maintaining a focus of high expectations for all learners by stating, "It is the responsibility of every educator working with every student to put in place the conditions and beliefs that he or she can, and will, learn at high levels" (p. 36). Teams can consider the needs of the student through the understanding of answering the question, "Will this student be expected to function independently when he or she leaves the public school system?" (Buffum, Mattos, & Weber, 2009). If the answer is yes, teams have a moral responsibility to ensure every effort is in place for the student to achieve content mastery. If the answer is no, teams need to have definitive evidence (such as cognitive or functional assessment or medical necessity) that the answer is, in fact, "no," and it's time for teams to begin personalizing the standards. Planning for students who may not be independent in life can be a complex process that deserves an entire book on how to best meet their learning needs. As special educators, the mindset of *all means all* carries through conversations and goal writing. It is the expectation that all students receiving IEPs will learn at high levels. As part of the student's IEP team, you accept the responsibility that grade-level content mastery is your responsibility. When teams create goals that are lower level, are not aligned to grade-level standards, and don't reflect the rigor of the highest levels of learning the student is capable of, it shows that the teams may not truly believe that all means all or they might not yet know how to create goals that show this.

Considering Two Critical Questions for Goals

In our work within the PLC process, we spent countless hours with school teams to select priority standards, determine common formative assessments, and then measure that progress toward grade-level standards. The collaborative teams and individuals for IEPs don't have to have the support of a PLC to do this work, but it must exist in some form as special education teams must have access to all this work to align their specially designed instruction toward the process of identifying goals.

Teams, for example, need to be able to successfully answer the first of the four critical questions of a PLC at Work: "What do we want students to know and be able to do?" (DuFour et al., 2024). This question extends to *all* students as this is grounded in the instruction on grade-level standards. This same level of focus and intentionality is wanted and needed for IEP goals. IEP teams, including the general education teacher, have to be able to answer this critical question, clearly articulating what they want *this* student to know and be able to do, aligned to the grade-level standard and based on their individual needs.

In addition, teams need to answer the second critical question, which is "How will we know if they learned it?" (DuFour et al., 2024). This question is addressed in chapter 6 (page 73). As stated in chapter 1 (page 13), both IDEA and the latest U.S. Supreme Court rulings determined through *Endrew F.*, that IEP-entitled students must have goals that are appropriately ambitious, and designed for a student to make growth. While the goals may differ, every student should have the chance to meet challenging objectives. This is demonstrated by creating goals that are *life-changing* for the student. Therefore, it's essential to maintain a steadfast approach of aligning IEP goals to grade-level standards and individualizing to alternative standards when necessary.

Writing Goals as a Team

Using the grade-level expectation as your target and the student's eligibility evaluation as your starting point, you will be able to determine areas where goals need to be developed. While the grade-level standard lets you know your destination and what steps to take to progress, the evaluation is just as vital to demonstrate how the student's disability impacts them. IEP goal areas may vary from state to state regarding what you are legally permitted to add to the IEP. Some states require an adverse impact statement included on the PLAAFP that specifically states where a goal can be developed in each academic or skill area. Other states allow any goal area once initial eligibility has been completed. Regardless, in the best interest of the student, teams must make data-informed decisions prior to developing any goal area. The team must have multiple data points to demonstrate how the student is impacted by the disability in the specific academic area instead of trying to provide specialized instruction simply because the student is already receiving services.

School-based teams have many options when it comes to goal writing, with the freedom to craft as many or as few goals as necessary. We urge you to be extremely intentional when crafting the student's goals, ensuring they are life-changing for the student. Planning a goal for a student that aligns with an essential grade-level standard ensures you are focusing on the most important areas. For example, a student may need specially designed instruction in reading comprehension. A goal could focus on the skill of answering comprehension questions about what the student read, or it could focus on putting pictures of the events that occurred from the story in order. Answering comprehension questions about what the student has read is a skill that crosses content areas and provides a depth or range of questions that can be built on throughout the school year, making this a more life-changing area for the team to focus their instruction. Teams should only write goals directly related to the student's area of eligibility. When determining how many goals to craft for a student, also consider when it is better to build team-based goals. A *team-based goal* is one that multiple providers support and track data toward progress. Team goals can be beneficial in a few different scenarios. Most often, they are implemented with a student who has multiple areas of need or a complex condition. Team goals can also be beneficial when related services and special education teachers partner together in supporting students through common goal areas. See figure 5.1 for a standards-aligned goal-planning tool to help with collaborative goal setting (the checks at the bottom are discussed in the next section on Writing Goals as an Individual, page 69).

Student Strengths (Present Levels, Classroom Data, and Previous Goal Data)

Strong sight word knowledge and recognition

Knows all sounds and blends

Previous goal to decode unfamiliar words met

NWEA MAP demonstrates strength in vocabulary and language

GORT assessment demonstrated weakness in sounds; goal data and classroom data show all sounds mastered

WADE assessment demonstrated weakness in nonsense words; goal data and classroom data show all sounds mastered

Able to answer basic recall questions (character, setting, place) after listening to a story read aloud

Figure 5.1: Standards-aligned goal-planning tool.

continued →

Student Challenges (Needs at Present Levels, Classroom Data, and Previous Goal Data)

Reading CFAs: Last three CFAs demonstrate level 1 (not meeting standard)

Assessment: Kaufman Test of Educational Achievement assessment demonstrated below fifth percentile in reading comprehension

NWEA MAP demonstrates consistently below tenth percentile in reading, with weakness in inferential text and literature

Reading benchmark assessments demonstrate difficulty with answering who, what, when, where questions about the text when student reads independently; unable to answer beyond the text questions at this time.

Priority Standards for Upcoming Grade Level Related to Goal Area

RL.5.1 Quote accurately from a text when explaining what the text says explicitly and when drawing inferences from the text.

Standard Unwrapped: Knowledge, Reasoning, or Skill (What does rigor and high levels of learning look like and sound like?)

- Grade-level text usage
- Accurate inference
- Identify where in text they found the information (collecting evidence)
- Independent work
- Inferences from pictures
- Inferences from emotions
- Inferences from actions in the story
- Inferences between two passages or two different stories

Proposed Goal

Within thirty-six instructional weeks (next annual review), when given a grade-level passage, Cindy will read the passage and cite text evidence to accurately identify (written or verbal) an inference in four out of five charted opportunities.

Benchmark or Objectives

By first reporting period, two out of five times

By second reporting period, three out of five times

By final reporting period, four out of five times

Goal Progression

Starting with where this student is according to present level through the priority standard for projected grade level. What is the specially designed instruction for this student?

Starting Point: Student is able to read 50 percent of the words in the passage (instructional level).
What does it mean to cite text evidence (explicit instruction and visual examples)?
What is an inference? Model out loud thinking (explicit instruction and visual examples).
Partner read an instructional grade-level and familiar passage and point to text evidence (highlight and use notes to keep place).
Listen to grade-level, familiar passage and create an inference (use two-column chart to write inferences).
Read an instructional grade-level passage and create an inference, citing text evidence (two-column chart inference and evidence).
Read an instructional grade-level passage and identify text evidence to build a storyline (storyline).
Read different genres of grade-level passage, identify text evidence, and state inferences (two-column chart and storylines).
End Goal: Read an on-grade level passage and create inference, citing text evidence.

Checks

Life-Changing: __X__   Stranger: __X__   So What: __X__   Lunchbox: __X__

Source for standard: National Governors Association Center for Best Practices & Council of Chief State School Officers, 2010b.

*Visit **go.SolutionTree.com/specialneeds** to download a free reproducible version of this figure.*

Team goals allow individuals with different lenses of expertise to collaborate to meet a student's needs. A few examples of some areas where team goals can be implemented include the following.

- Reading and language (general education teacher, special education teacher, speech-language pathologist)
    + Reading comprehension and answering questions
    + Reading comprehension and language use
    + Reading fluency and sound accuracy
- Mathematics and problem solving (general education teacher, special education teacher, occupational therapist)
    + Solving multistep problems and visual tracking
- Writing
    + Composition and formation shared between the special education teacher and the occupational therapist
    + Composition and language expression shared between the special education teacher and speech-language pathologist

- Executive functioning
    + Creating and following a multistep plan to complete an assignment or activity shared between the special education teacher, occupational therapist, and counselor
    + Starting and completing a task shared between special education teacher, counselor, and occupational therapist
    + Following multistep directions shared between special education teacher, counselor, occupational therapist, and speech-language pathologist
    + Organization shared between special education teacher, counselor, occupational therapist, and speech-language pathologist
- Coping skills and body awareness
    + Handling frustration shared between special education teacher and counselor
    + Recognizing body awareness (sensory) shared between occupational therapist, counselor, and special education teacher
    + Asking for and taking a break shared between occupational therapist, counselor, and special education teacher

While these are some examples, it is not a comprehensive list. The greatest value in teams collaborating and sharing goals is that it allows for a few key wins for the student, such as multiple providers reinforcing the same concepts, repeated opportunities for demonstrating mastery, and a variety of expertise in providing instruction. What can happen when teams aren't sharing goals is that different providers work in isolation toward a specific skill. This misses the opportunity to reinforce across the multitude of settings and is a splintered approach. When teams work as a collaborative group and share goal ownership, it allows for higher levels of intentionality and success through a combined effort across the different areas the student is exposed to during the day. Likewise, when possible, it is the same as when school teams and private or home-based teams are able to collaborate and support the same skills using similar methods. The level of intentionality and focus for the student demonstrates much higher success and growth. In thinking of the road trip analogy, when teams collaborate and use team goals, it allows for the trip to be more efficient. For example, when you stop to get gas, you want to stretch, get snacks, and use the facilities, all at the same stop. Stopping to get gas, then stopping to stretch, and then stopping yet again for snacks, and once again to use the facilities takes valuable time away from getting to the destination. Collaborating with the same goal in mind allows you to be much more specialized and intentional with your focus.

Writing Goals as an Individual

There are times when we have to craft goals in isolation due to the student's needs and that is OK. You never want to force a goal area to be a team goal if it isn't in the best interest of the student. When writing goals where there will only be one specialist working on the goal, it is vital that you collaborate with the general education teacher on the goal. In the end, the general education teacher is often with the student for longer periods of the day and has the general education content specialty knowledge of what the grade level looks like, so it is imperative that they are also a contributor. Solo goals should be just as intentional as team goals, created with extensive collaboration with the general education teacher.

IEP teams can often find themselves creating multiple goals for students and asking themselves, "How many goals are enough?" The simple answer is we need enough to provide the appropriate support for the student. That can become more difficult when breaking down each area a student may struggle with in a specific area. For example, with all the different components of reading, do you focus on fluency, accuracy, comprehension, recall, inferring, predicting, or character analysis? In short, teams should craft goals based on the deficit areas identified in the evaluation and the prioritized standards. This is where the collaboration with the general education teacher plays a major role in helping to identify what is the largest priority area and how that impacts the student. Teams can use the IEP goal checklist in figure 5.2 to determine if they have crafted the right goals. We will focus on the first four goals in this book.

Stranger check	Can anyone pick up this goal, read it, understand it, teach it, and collect data on it?	☐
Lunchbox check	Can a lunchbox complete this task?	☐
So what? check	So what? How will completing this goal improve their education and skills?	☐
Life-changing check	Is this goal so important that it is worthy of spending time working toward? Will it drastically change the student's learning experience?	☐
Data collection check	Can anyone collect data on this goal? Is the end result of the goal clear to everyone?	☐
Grade-level check	Is this goal aligned to the student's grade level? Is there an appropriate learning progression in place?	☐

Figure 5.2: IEP goal checklist.

Stranger Check

The *stranger check* is one of the easiest for teams to use. The check goes like this: if a stranger picked up this goal, would they be able to read the goal, understand what the goal means and what is being taught, and be able to collect measurable data on the goal? In an ever-changing world, the mobility rates of students have increased drastically as has the amount of staff turnover, especially within special education. We can never assume that what we thought we intended when we crafted the goal is clear to anyone who picks up the IEP. For example, in partnership with the family, we want to ensure that the family has complete understanding of what their child is working on at school toward their IEP. When we use abbreviations, specific program tools, or educational jargon, we are not always meeting the stranger test. When we use goal statements, such as "... will achieve level M on F&P ..." or "... have 80 percent accuracy on IXL," these statements do not specifically say what the student needs to do to meet the goals, only what the measure will be for progress. Instead, goals should demonstrate the skills or strategies of that specific expectation, such as, "After reading a grade-level text, ... will answer within the text and beyond the text comprehension questions such as but not limited to. ..."

Lunchbox Check

Next, we have the *lunchbox check*. Many times, behavior analysts will use this test to determine behavior. However, it is something that we can all implement regarding our goals. Essentially, the *lunchbox check* means that if a lunchbox can perform this goal, it needs to be changed to something that demonstrates a skill or active engagement from the student. Goals that don't meet the lunchbox check are typically indicated by using *will not* or *won't*. They focus on a skill or activity the student will stop doing. Some abbreviated examples of goals that *won't* pass the lunchbox check would be, "Student will not leave the classroom without permission" or "Student will not engage in tantrums for seven minutes" (a lunchbox can achieve either one of these goals). To address these goals, teams need to focus on what behavior or skill we want the student to demonstrate rather than focus on what we don't want the student to be doing. A better option is, "Student will ask for and wait for permission to transition to another location" or "Student will ask for a break or use a coping strategy from their menu."

So What? Check

The third check when writing goals focuses on *so what?* In the event the student is able to complete this skill, so what? Basically, the goal should be vital for devoting the time to completing the task. After reading the goal, it should be clear why it is important for the student to be working on this rather than working on anything else. Sometimes, we like to think of this as the *yes* goal, meaning that if you say yes to this goal, it means you are saying no to other things that could be addressed. Therefore, the goal must pass the so what? check to demonstrate why it is important and necessary to focus on this goal at this time. An example of a goal that would not pass the so what? check is, "When writing a sentence, student will have a period at the end of each sentence." Yes, punctuation is vital for writing and reading, yet are we going to spend an entire year only working on putting a period at the end of the sentence? So what? goals are typically low rigor and demonstrate low achievement because they aren't reaching for something substantial or high levels of complexity.

Life-Changing Check

Finally, the most important goal check is the *life-changing check*, which is one that teams sometimes feel the most uncomfortable addressing. Does this goal demonstrate something that will change this student's life for the better? When we look at goals, we want the goal to be meaningful, and the thought of the student being unable to meet the goal would have devastating consequences. It's the difference between a student who can advocate for what they need or how they are feeling instead of a student who can match predetermined feelings on a chart. A life-changing goal for reading is when a student can understand the text and complete complex character analysis versus identifying the main character in the passage. The goal will be so massively life-changing that you may worry what would happen if the goal isn't met. The IEP goals agreed on at the meeting are what the team will spend their time focusing on throughout the upcoming year, which means they better be well worth the time and will impact the student for the better and change their educational future.

Conclusion

When you think about the goal section of our travel road trip, our goals determine our progress along our trip. You may write a goal to achieve so many miles in one day or to make it to a specific destination where a comfy hotel bed is waiting. Just like our goal for the IEP, you want to ensure your travel goals pass your checkpoints. Do you know how far you are trying to go today? Do you all know our destination? Is it possible to achieve this if you work together? This mainly means you aren't stopping every thirty minutes just because a passenger is bored. When you remain intentional on your journey to reach your daily endpoint, you may be able to relax a moment before bed or even visit the gym and pool!

In special education, you do not require job security to keep your customers. The greatest service you can do for your students and your school is to create learning environments where you are not needed, and students are able to independently access the general education setting. It is most satisfying when teams are able to evaluate and determine that goal areas aren't needed or that even the IEP isn't needed any longer. That is a job well done in special education. Less than 3 percent of students are dismissed from special education annually (National Center for Education Statistics, 2021). We have to ask ourselves, "Why are we not closing this gap? Why have we not been successful in our efforts?" We make many different rationales for why students aren't dismissed from services more frequently. If we are examining our practices, it often comes down to the fact that our goals aren't driven to closing the gap at high levels and that we aren't providing the right, individualized supports for the specific student needs. As teams, we have a huge mountain to climb; however, with the right collaboration and instructional intentionality, we can start to climb that mountain.

Now that we understand the various points that go into building goals, in chapter 6, we will examine further how to use the present levels in crafting goals that are aligned to grade-level standards. We will also look at the final piece of goals and identify how we measure the progress toward the goal, answering the second critical question, "How will we know they know?"

Chapter 5 Reflection

Do your IEP goals pass these four checks: Stranger? Lunchbox? So what? Life-changing?

Red Light Areas	**Yellow Light Areas**	**Green Light Areas**
Identify practices that must stop	Identify essential actions to take	Identify actions to continue

CHAPTER 6
WRITING GOALS: DATA CONSIDERATIONS

The principle goal of education is to create individuals who are capable of doing new things, not simply repeating what other generations have done.

—Jean Piaget

Collaborative teams have many different options for writing goals. Within special education, teams often spend a large majority of their time on the black-and-white legal requirements of goals without spending time focusing beyond this into the gray area of goal writing. Compliance conversations focus on dates, data, and alignment to evaluation as required by IDEA and state governance. We often share there is, in fact, no "IEP jail" that violators go to when their IEP breaks the law. However, state boards of education, attorneys, advocates, and families will question IEPs, and they have due process rights. Therefore, just because teams won't be jailed over an IEP, it is important that they work together collaboratively to build an appropriate IEP that is designed to support the student.

If the *Endrew F.* case taught us anything, it is that the U.S. Supreme Court can intervene and case law changes. When this happens, we do not want to be on the other side of an IEP asking what you should've, would've, or could've done differently. When the IEP is questioned or when the team disagrees on the goals, the team needs to make decisions based on data while also maintaining high expectations of learning. When we believe that all means *all* and that it is our collective responsibility to ensure we are teaching for content mastery, our IEP goals must be crafted with intentionality for learning. Lucky for us as members of a collaborative team, we are relentless in challenging the status quo, and as one of our core commitments, we believe that all students can learn at high levels. Even more importantly, we value data and use student data to inform our instruction, including within special education teams. These data and our beliefs in high achievement for all allow us to create IEPs that have goals rooted in data and aligned to high levels of instruction, which are defendable when challenged.

In the last chapter, we focused on the importance of why we need collaborative goals; in chapter 1 (page 13), we discussed how writing IEPs since *Endrew F.* has drastically changed where the new baseline of providing special education instruction begins. Therefore, make sure that teams are writing goals to the highest of student growth, ensuring they are life-changing for the student by designing them to close the gap with the highest levels of intensity. Student IEP goals must be written so there is a clear progression from where the student is currently performing to where the student will be within a year as a result of the specially designed instruction provided by the team. This chapter discusses the present levels of performance (PLOP), when to use benchmarks or objectives, finalizing the writing of life-changing goals, and how to use the four critical questions of a PLC. Even if you're not an official PLC, you can make effective use of the critical questions for this work.

Writing the Present Level of Performance

Some would argue the present level of performance is the most important part of the IEP. We agree that it is one of the two most important parts of the IEP (together with the PLAAFP). A present level of performance that is data-driven combined with a life-changing goal is vital for intentional student growth. A solid PLOP section is necessary so that everyone reading the IEP and working with the student knows and understands exactly where the student is beginning for this goal area, creating a baseline to later build your goal progression. In chapter 5 (page 61), we discussed the essentials of creating a life-changing goal, which is built from solid, data-driven present levels as your baseline. A well-written PLOP contains an accurate and thorough description of the specific skills the student has related to this goal. When a PLOP is well-defined, the teachers know the exact coordinates of the starting point. The PLOP should give enough data-based information so that the reader is able to almost predict what the goal area will be and have a full understanding of how the student is presently demonstrating their knowledge in this specific area. The following is an example.

> Dan's latest performance on his grade-level assessments demonstrates a strength in solving addition word problems independently. On his last four assessments, he achieved 100 percent on the addition word problems within 100. When he has to determine if the word problem is addition or subtraction, he is accurate approximately 50 percent of the time. Dan can identify the math words in the word problem; however, he mixes up the addition and subtraction words. When solving subtraction word problems within 50, he accurately solves 40 percent of problems with difficulties when he has to borrow. Typical second graders are able to solve word problems with mixed operations (addition and subtraction) within 100 independently.

Teams that do not spend enough time ensuring the PLOP is accurate and well-written can find themselves in a precarious place. Common pitfalls of poorly written PLOPs result in teams having inconsistent information or unclear directions to where the goal is working toward or what is being worked on through the goal. The following are some key examples for teams to review and determine how they can adjust their present levels.

- PLOPs that use vague statements that speak in broad generalizations such as "struggles with reading," "personal area of need in mathematics," "reading below grade level," or "reading at a level M." These statements don't demonstrate the specific skills that the student is working toward. A better statement would describe exactly what skills the student has already achieved and what their deficit areas are in relation to this area: "Cindy is able to identify the first fifty sight words of first grade and all fifty sight words in the kindergarten curriculum. She is able to identify fifty to seventy-five sight words with 50 percent accuracy. She struggles to generalize reading these words in sentences. She can identify the words on flashcards; however, she cannot identify them in the passages. End-of-first-grade expectations are to identify all 150 sight words (both kindergarten and first-grade lists)."

- PLOPs that do not match the present levels of academic achievement and functional performance are confusing and problematic. If you recall, the PLAAFP (page 47) is at the beginning of the IEP and covers all areas of instruction, while the PLOP is specific to this goal area. Parents and guardians, attorneys, advocates, and others will gravitate to any discrepancy between the two, which often occurs when teams are not working together or considering all the data when they begin to write goals. Teams will input the academic data on the PLAAFP with grades, district assessments, and so on, but they may not consider this same data when writing the PLOP. The PLAAFP page contains more of a full, comprehensive summary and, when required, the PLOP on the individual goal page needs to be specific to the goal statement area. There should be a direct correlation between the PLAAFP and the PLOP. The PLAAFP is created for the larger overview, and the PLOP is specific to the particular goal. The two should complement each other in demonstrating what the student is able to complete. Remember, we consider the PLOP as the starting data point for your IEP goal, so this is essential, and the goal should be well-written and defined with data. Teams need to ensure they provide clear information. Avoid stating that a student was "average" or within "average ranges" on a district standardized assessment on one page and then reporting the student is struggling on another page. Similar problems also can occur when everyone on the team is not collaborating on goals. For example, when a service team member reports a student is struggling with a specific skill, the classroom or special education teacher reports that skill as mastered or at grade level.

- PLOPs that don't contain relevant and specific data become opinions. Therefore, the PLOP should contain a statement demonstrating what the general education expectations are concerning this area. Teams must demonstrate that they are working toward grade- or age-level expectations.

A PLOP that is crafted with details based on specific data to demonstrate exactly what the student can perform currently with and without support lays a solid foundation for the goal area. The PLOP needs to include enough information to understand exactly where the student is in relation to the proposed goal as well as what a typical peer would be expected to complete. Remember, a well-written PLOP is the pinpoint of the specific map coordinates of your starting location rather than the generalized city. It would be confusing to tell someone you are leaving from Chicago rather than you are leaving from Wrigley Field, 1060 W Addison St., Chicago, Illinois, which is at the corner of Addison and Clark facing south. The amount of detail that you have allows you to chart your path to begin your adventure, which gives you more intentionality to plan your route. This is the level of specificity teams need to create when they are writing their present levels.

A PLOP for a reading comprehension goal may look like the following.

> *Fifth-grader Taylor is able to fluently read grade-level fiction and nonfiction texts. He is able to retell a story when provided with a storyline to complete, and he is able to answer questions about the setting and main idea of the passage in a fiction text. In a nonfiction text, Taylor can identify the time order and sequence of events with visual support. He struggles to answer inferential questions and to identify character traits in a fiction text. A fifth-grade expectation for students is to be able to compare and contrast characters from two different passages as well as to infer the ending of a passage based on details within the passage.*

Having a well-written PLOP allows the team to know, specific to this goal area only, the student's strengths, needed areas for improvement, and the most recent results of assessments related to the goal area for the district and the classroom. The PLOP is your starting point for this goal and includes the data that support how the team will know where the student is presently specific to the goal.

When teams have invested the pre-work to build a strong data-based present level, the goal will help to identify the next logical steps based on the student's starting point and the grade-level standard that the student is working to demonstrate mastery. This work is best completed in conjunction with the general education teacher. Together, you can build a goal that represents both the grade-level rigor and the student's individual learning needs. For schools and districts that operate as a PLC or have similarly aligned collaborative practices they adhere to, general education teachers invest a large amount of time building learning progressions that align with the grade-level standards and demonstrating sequential steps toward obtaining these. For schools that don't already have priority standards or learning progressions already established, this work becomes more challenging. We suggest these teams explore professional development in texts such as *Learning by Doing* (DuFour et al., 2024) or *Taking Action* (Mattos et al., 2025) to get further information on these topics. When special education teachers embark on this process with general education teams to craft IEP goals that have the highest levels of leverage and endurance, it helps the student build grade-level standard competencies and deeper levels of understanding.

As teams begin the work of determining what standard has the most leverage to create specially designed instruction toward crafting and achieving the IEP goal, it is essential to map out the learning plan for the student through the IEP goal. Begin with determining the student's baseline starting point. Once the baseline data are reviewed, combine classroom information from the general education teacher and the special education teacher, and then the team reviews the selected grade-level standard and crafts a personalized learning progression to meet grade-level mastery through specially designed instruction. Using the earlier example from Dan (page 74), let's build a logical goal progression for him as an example.

PLOP or Baseline

Dan's latest performance on his grade-level assessments demonstrates a strength in solving addition word problems independently. On his last four assessments, he achieved 100 percent on the addition word problems within 100. When he has to determine if the word problem is addition or subtraction, he is accurate approximately 50 percent of the time. Dan can identify the math words in the word problem; however, he mixes up the addition and subtraction words. When solving subtraction word problems within 50, he accurately solves 40 percent of problems, with difficulties when he has to borrow. Typical second graders are able to solve word problems with mixed operations (addition and subtraction) within 100 independently.

Third-grade priority standard (for next school year when this IEP will end) is the following:

Use multiplication and division within 100 to solve word problems in situations involving equal groups, arrays, and measurement quantities, e.g., by using drawings and equations with a symbol for the unknown number to represent the problem (3.OA.A3; National Governors Association Center for Best Practices & Council of Chief State School Officers, 2010b).

Proposed Goal

By the annual review of 2025, given a word problem within 100 with mixed operations (addition, subtraction, multiplication, division), Dan will use a strategy to determine the correct operation and solve with 80 percent accuracy in 4/5 charted opportunities.

Goal Progression

- Correctly identify key words to determine operation.
- Correctly complete addition and subtraction (outside of word problems) with and without regrouping.
- Solve for addition within 100.
- Solve for subtraction within 50 with and without regrouping.
- Solve for subtraction within 100 with and without regrouping.
- Solve for addition or subtraction within 100.
- Solve for multiplication within 100.
- Solve for addition, subtraction, or multiplication within 100.
- Solve for division within 100.
- Solve for addition, subtraction, multiplication, or division within 100.

Determining When to Use Benchmarks or Objectives

Just like in planning what route to take on your road trip, plan your route for how to deliver targeted specially designed instruction to reach your end goal. Teams need to plan from the baseline through to the end goal and determine the logical learning progression that would provide for the student to reach the goal. Therefore, create a course that ensures guaranteed access to the general education expectations through the delivery of our intentional instruction. When planning an IEP goal, you sometimes need to determine the fastest route possible and ensure you have the foundational skills to be successful in finishing the route the fastest.

Now that the team has a clearly defined starting point (baseline) and ending point (aligned to grade-level standard) for the goal, the next crucial part of the goal writing process needs to occur, which is determining your benchmarks or objectives and the logical steps needed for achieving the goal. While the terms may be used interchangeably, there is a large difference between writing benchmarks or objectives.

It is up to the team to determine if the goals are benchmarks or objectives based on the individual student's needs. Teams must consider not only what the goal will be but how they will be providing the specially designed instruction toward the goal and how they will track the data of this instruction to decide between benchmarks or objectives. If the planned instruction is sequential, it makes sense to complete benchmarks that change in number. As an example, a goal that progresses from 50–60 percent to 70–80 percent accuracy is a *benchmark*. If the instruction features different aspects to be addressed, it makes more sense to complete objectives. For example, a goal that focuses on multiple skills all at once, such as asking for a break, using a learned strategy, and implementing the strategy independently, is an *objective*.

Some states require written benchmarks or objectives to be a part of the IEP, other states only require these for students who are on alternative pathways, and some states do not require them at all. Each district creates its requirements based on the individual state requirements and its own legal representation's advice. Even if your state does not require written benchmarks or objectives within the IEP, teams need to ensure the goals they are proposing have logical learning progressions and skill demonstrations intentionally planned throughout the year. In addition, benchmarks or objectives allow teams to measure progress and inform their teaching of what strategies work and what strategies need to be revisited.

When to Use Benchmarks

Benchmark-style goals work great for reading fluency with words per minute, mathematics computation, accuracy-based goals, or behavior goals for skill improvement. These types of goals build on each other in a numerical fashion, such as 80 words correct per minute, 100 words correct per minute, then 120 words correct per minute, or 60 percent accuracy, 70 percent accuracy, then 80 percent accuracy. Benchmark-based goals begin with your student's baseline and build toward how many steps are needed to reach the end goal throughout the year. Therefore, for the first step when writing benchmarks and creating a progression of skills that builds on each prior skill, you will need to determine what the rate of improvement will be for the student to know where you will have your benchmarks. For example, benchmarks can be viewed as ladders of sequential skill progression with each skill building on the previous one, such as a counting goal from 1 to 40, breaking it down by counting 1 to 10, then 1 to 20, then 1 to 30, and finally 1 to 40.

When to Use Objectives

Objectives can be used for all types of goal areas, such as reading comprehension or mathematics problem solving. They can also be used for executive functioning and behavior improvement goals. Objective-based goals work on building all the concepts of an academic skill throughout the year. One of the larger rationales for using objective-based goals is to ensure you are developing ongoing concepts, such as reading comprehension skills of answering questions after reading or hearing a passage based on within-the-text, beyond-the-text, and about-the-text skill sets. As a student progresses through the reading levels, each of these areas needs to be addressed. Therefore, the team needs to build on and review them throughout the year rather than focus only on one and then move on to the next. In some cases, objective-based goals allow teams more flexibility to align toward grade-level units and the provision of services that are more naturally embedded within the general education classrooms.

Finalizing the Writing of Life-Changing Goals

Regardless of whether you are formally including written benchmarks or objectives in your IEP goal, or if you are using them as progress determination stages toward mastery, what is most important is that the team has reviewed the starting point, has planned out how the student will progress based on the specially designed instruction they are provided, and knows what the year-end goal will be according to the grade-level standard. The amount of benchmarks or objectives created needs to be determined based on the individual student and what makes the most educational impact for the student. Remember, we are looking for life-changing goals! Going beyond what is required on the IEP paperwork, teams need to ensure they have a solid plan with an understanding of what appropriate progress looks like, outlining intentional instruction to close the learning gap throughout the next year, and how they will measure the student's growth before the IEP is finalized.

Implementing Goal Data Collection

Teams also must agree on how they are measuring success before they begin to implement the goal. Without having a full understanding of how to measure the success of the goal, you miss the opportunity to ensure you are being intentional about what you are working toward. One of the goal tests from chapter 5 (page 61) is the stranger check, which means that anyone who picks up the IEP can read the goal and understand exactly what the goal is working toward and exactly how the goal is being measured. It may be beneficial for teams to have an agreed-on structure for data collection. This specific method or tool should be shared at the IEP meeting so that everyone has a full understanding of not only what the goal is, but also how the team will be collecting the vital data to determine the student's progress. Teams have many choices in how they will measure progress. For example, progress can be measured using number of trials, percentage of accuracy, number of words read correctly, number of attempts, or a variety of other options. Determining the data collection method and tool is the final step in creating a student goal. The writing of the goal isn't completed until the team agrees on the data collection tool. It is the final touches on the goal that allow for the last checkpoints to determine if the teams wrote an ambitious goal and have a plan for how they are providing the instruction and how they know if it is working.

Using the Critical Questions of a PLC

As we introduced in chapter 5 (page 61), even if your school or district doesn't operate as a PLC, the collaborative work around IEPs that you do as teams of educators will benefit from the implementation of the four critical questions of a PLC. Teams must create IEP goals to answer with specificity the first two questions: What do we want this student to know and be able to do? and How will we know when they learned it? (DuFour et al., 2024). Often, even in established PLCs, teams consider the four critical questions as only related to general education studies; however, the questions are very much a part of providing special education instruction, and teams need to review these with the same level of intensity when building units of study. All teams need to understand the necessity of ensuring that IEP goals are legally binding and created with a degree of intensity to ensure that teachers are held to the highest levels of rigor. Their designated plan outlines how their instruction is going to build the student's skills toward success.

Occasionally, goal data don't always demonstrate the progress that teams had anticipated for the student. Therefore, it is essential to focus on the third critical question: How will we respond when students do not learn? (DuFour et al., 2024). When the data show a stall or not as much progress as planned, it is important that teams intervene immediately and determine the next best steps to right the course. On a road trip, this would be a detour or an accident on the road. Do you have enough data to alter the course? Do you need to give it a little bit of time for the problem to clear up? Or do you need to go back and try a different route?

Teams need to always remember that clearly defined plans and intentional instruction set the framework for success; however, even the best plans sometimes need to be altered or restructured to meet student needs, and that is OK. Be responsive to what the student demonstrates and what the data show. It doesn't always mean that you must start over or rewrite the goal. It means you need to look at what is currently successful, where there are current struggles, and how you can provide something different. Some questions teams might want to consider include the following.

- Where was the student successful?
- How are we using the student's strength areas?
- Is there a foundational skill we need to go back and revisit so that we can be successful?
- Do we need to look at how we are structuring the task or the expectation?
- Is there a different way the student can demonstrate the knowledge?
- Is it the setting or topic we are providing for the instruction or collecting the data?
- Are there other things like executive functioning, attention, or behavior that are hindering the progress toward the goal?

When teams come across the need to review the plan and notice that they need to revisit their instruction, it isn't a bad thing because they rely on data to ensure their instruction is making the progress expected. Educational teams that are in tune with the student data and progress can identify when a student's progress starts to slow. Therefore, the teams are responsive by making educational adjustments to help the student continue to make progress.

While it's easy to focus on overcoming inevitable challenges in meeting goals, teams must also consider how to react to success, hence the fourth critical question: How will we extend learning for students who have learned it? (DuFour et al., 2024). Make no mistake, your students will experience success right along with any challenges, so you need to have plans in place for what's next. As a collaborative team, when you are building out the individualized goal learning progression, it is important to consider planning *to* and *through* the standard you are aligning. Just like when preparing for your road trip, you always plan to have enough gas or snacks to make the trip; similarly, you want to ensure you have built your plan to include opportunities for extension to be prepared to seize the moment and continue instruction meaningfully.

To answer both the third and fourth critical questions, teams continually look at the data they gather throughout the entire year, adjusting or restructuring along the way to inform their subsequent instruction and strategies. They review the progress each week, and when it is time to formally update goals, the data are extremely familiar to them, with examples and artifacts that demonstrate how the goal has been addressed throughout.

Conclusion

When teams are all on the same level of understanding of the goal area, the final piece is to determine how they will maintain a collaborative framework for instruction. It can become easy for everyone to agree on the goal and feel wonderful about the outcome; however, we have to ensure that we are continually sharing the instructional responsibility for the student's learning. To help with this, teams may want to consider how they are sharing updates and strategies that are working or not as successful as they had intended. While dedicated collaborative planning time is ideal between the special education teacher and general education teacher, a shared instructional plan is a vital source of two-way communication between general education and special education. At a minimum, the instructional plan needs to identify what the current standard and skill being addressed is, what strategies are being implemented, and how both teachers are working toward success.

Now that you have your car packed, and your route to your destination, you need to determine how you are going to get there comfortably. We all know that road trips can be long and at times boring, but having the right company, the right playlist, and the right snacks helps. In the next chapter, we will dive into how the student's accommodations and modifications support the student within the school and how to ensure they fit the student, are necessary, and are essential to the student's success.

Chapter 6 Reflection

When creating student IEP goals, how do we collect data and build goal progressions?

Red Light Areas	**Yellow Light Areas**	**Green Light Areas**
Identify practices that must stop	Identify essential actions to take	Identify actions to continue

CHAPTER 7

UNDERSTANDING ACCOMMODATIONS AND MODIFICATIONS

*The beautiful thing about learning
is nobody can take it away from you.*

—B. B. King

IDEA requires school teams to create an IEP that not only provides the present levels (PLAAFP) and annual goals (PLOP and standards-aligned goal) to support the student. Teams also must include the necessary accommodations and modifications necessary for the student to access their educational environment. While the terms *accommodations* and *modifications* are often lumped together in conversation, they serve very different purposes in supporting students. One of the most important questions in our interview process for new staff is having a potential staff member articulate the difference between an accommodation and a modification and explain how to determine the need for either. This chapter will discuss what accommodations and modifications are, the best practices for specifying them, and why it is essential to use data to inform what they are.

Exploring Accommodations and Modifications

According to IDEA (2004), an accommodation is an adaptation or change to the environment that allows a student to overcome the impact of the challenges they face due to their disability. Accommodations that are appropriately used address the individual barriers preventing the student from achieving full access within the educational environment and do not have an impact on or change *what* the student is learning. Accommodations focus on *how* students are able to access their learning while not changing the rigor or the content of the instruction.

When teams are looking to implement a *modification*, they are looking to alter or change the instruction the student is receiving or the curriculum the student is exposed to within the general education setting. Modifications are a change to *what* the student is learning and oftentimes result in a significant change in the curriculum and expectation. Teams look to modifications after all options for accommodations and instructional strategies have been exhausted, but the student still requires a significant modification to the instruction to be successful.

To determine what types of support the student needs, teams must take an individual approach that is based on a few different data points. First, what does the evaluation for special education determine the student requires as a result of how their disability impacts them in the different educational environments? Second, what do the current data show in regard to the student's level of independence and how they are currently accessing instruction throughout the school day? Review the data from a variety of areas within the student's day, including the general education classrooms, structured and unstructured settings, levels of independence, as well as transitions within the school day when necessary.

The best intentions for accommodations and modifications can sometimes create a more restrictive environment than students need to demonstrate their skills. During the IEP meeting, determining accommodations and modifications can remind us of shopping in preparation for the road trip. There is no budget. There is no shopping list. It is literally about what looks or sounds good or that we think could be needed throughout the journey. One of two things happens after we start the trip. All the best food is eaten right away. If hardly any of the food is eaten, additional stops are needed to get better snacks. We wonder why the snacks that looked so perfect in the store don't work for us as we drive to our destination. Accommodations and modifications can be the same way. During the IEP meeting, a multitude of items can be added *just in case*. This problem can happen when the team doesn't collaborate well or meaningfully determine what is necessary and can be implemented.

Specifying Accommodations

Collaborative teams discuss not only the student's present levels and goals, but also what data they have on how the student is using the supports and what is working and necessary to continue. Team-recommended accommodations go beyond good teaching practices, such as repeating directions or checking in to ensure the student is on task, preferred seating, and so on. Teams propose specific accommodations based on their current data about how the student's disability impacts them to access the learning in their setting. Specific accommodations for the individual student reflect how the information is presented to the student or how the student is going to respond to the information, such as providing speech-to-text for written responses beyond three sentences; allowing preferred seating away from the air conditioning and vents to reduce background noise; breaking assignments down into first, next, then; providing a worked example or model for multistep problems; and testing in a small group of no more than seven with stop-the-clock breaks after every fifteen minutes of testing.

Teams that dive deep into truly knowing how the student performs across a variety of settings are able to provide specific accommodations that are reflective of how the student is performing so that anyone who reads the IEP knows precisely what this student requires to be successful. Avoid vague accommodation phrasings, such as preferred seating, small group, offer breaks, and chunk assignments (see table 7.1). When drafting the IEP and proposing accommodations to the team, everyone needs to remember that accommodations are required supports that ensure the student's access within the general education settings is successful despite how their disability affects them.

Table 7.1: Accommodation Phrasing

Vague Language	Specific Language
Preferential seating	Provide seating away from the door, facing the board.
Additional time	Student can request additional time to complete an assignment of time and a half.
Repeat directions	Check with student for understanding of directions.

Specifying Modifications

Modifications serve a much different purpose than accommodations. Properly determined modifications have a goal that works toward eliminating the need for the modification. When reviewing the individual student data, teams must ensure they are providing the necessary instruction and support for the student and avoid modifications that unintentionally reduce rigor. Modifications must be explicit about when they are used and to what degree the instructional materials need to be altered to ensure that teachers hold students to high expectations while allowing them to demonstrate their understanding. Appropriate modifications are based on how the student is impacted by their disability and include strategies, such as using a textbook or novel at the instructional decoding level while assessing the grade-level comprehension strategy or reducing the number of questions for a student who demonstrates a limited amount of time to focus (table 7.2, page 88). Modifications can also be used to permit a student to select an answer from a field of three instead of from a field of five for reading comprehension if a student has a significant processing delay.

Table 7.2: Comparing Types of Modifications and Accommodations

Modifications	Accommodations
Lower grade-level materials	Additional time when requested
Alternative curriculum	Student reads material aloud
Reducing rigor	Headphones when testing to block out distractions
Reduced amount of questions	Reduced material on a page for visual clarity

Using Data to Inform Accommodations and Modifications

When recommending any sort of accommodation or modification, each member of the team must understand the data collected to support the accommodations and modifications and what the data look like across the school setting. The educational team needs to ensure that it is consistent in how it supports the student and how it collects data on the use of these supports. When teams don't collaborate, this becomes evident in the accommodations and modifications because the general education partners are most often the ones responsible for the implementation. When there is a lack of communication and collaboration, you may see accommodations recommended that are either (1) not possible for the general education teacher to implement, or (2) not necessary based on the student's needs. Collaboration between team members on how the student is currently performing, as well as data around the need for accommodations, helps to ensure the right recommendations are made and implemented. This collaboration also allows for an opportunity for the general education teacher and special education teacher to have an open conversation regarding *how* these supports will be implemented throughout the student's school day. Therefore, the team needs to ensure it creates a plan that everyone helped build and that can be implemented. Too often, we come across IEPs with fifteen- to twenty-plus accommodations and modifications included for the student. How is it possible for the general education teacher to implement all of these with fidelity? Unfortunately, they can't and don't. Teams are asking for the impossible if they expect long lists of accommodations to be implemented without thoughtful planning on how to support the student within the general education environment. Teams should begin with a collaborative conversation, beginning with the student's strength areas and bridging into the areas where the evaluation and current data demonstrate the student has areas to support. Look closely to determine how the student's disability impacts their progress in the school environment and what is expected of their same-grade peers.

Determining the necessary accommodations and modifications for assessments is also a collaborative team discussion that is data-informed. Teams should be sure to provide a consistent level of support from the classroom through district and state testing. The team's responsibility is to provide the student with the right support and strategies to create an environment for the student to demonstrate their knowledge consistently. As part of their collaborative discussion, teams need to consider what is permitted for district and state testing and how they are teaching the students to use necessary strategies on classroom assessments to prepare for a similar testing environment. For example, teams might want to create a testing accommodation that allows the student to demonstrate their work on a thinking map or graphic organizer for classroom-based assessments, which also may be a terrific way for the student to organize their thoughts and demonstrate their knowledge. However, we can't provide this accommodation for a district or state assessment. Teams should then collaborate to teach the student how to create an organizer themselves using the strategies they have learned throughout the year. Teams can model how to draw the organizer and fill it in, rather than just providing the organizer for students to complete. In other words, teams must spend the time to help the student understand not just the content but how to use an appropriate strategy to demonstrate their knowledge of the content resulting in ownership of their learning.

Well-meaning teams who provide accommodations and modifications without data to inform the needs are creating environments where educators don't allow students to learn at their highest levels and can create low expectations for them. In addition, adding accommodations and modifications from a *just in case* perspective without intentionally teaching the student skills or specific strategies to use creates an environment that can't always be replicated as the student grows. For example, imagine a student has a specific learning disability related to reading decoding and word retrieval, and the team has implemented the following supports: (1) a comprehension test is read aloud with a familiar adult in a separate one-on-one setting, and (2) the student is allowed to explain their answer verbally. This well-intentioned team shared that the student needs to have the test read to them. This support ensures they are being assessed on the content based on the data that the student often substitutes words with the same beginning letters and then would answer incorrectly. The team also shared that the student needs a separate one-on-one setting to avoid disturbing the other students and that the student does better with familiar adults when they are explaining their answers. While these may all be true statements, how is the team helping the student to articulate their knowledge regardless of who they are testing with? Is it always necessary to test one-on-one and have an adult read the test? Can technology be used to read the test to the student in the classroom using headphones so the student can learn to test in the same environment as their peers? How are we preparing this student to take district and state assessments where this may not be an acceptable accommodation? Even more important, how are we preparing them for success later in life?

Teams that support populations, such as multilingual learners, students using assistive technology, or students with low-incidence disabilities, need to remember that all members of the team are part of the collaboration in building student accommodations and modifications. Therefore, ensure that all teachers involved in a student's learning—be that the general education teacher, special education teacher, EL teacher, or others—all collaborate on how to support the student's needs. For example, students who use assistive technology for their augmentative communication have much different needs than students who use assistive technology for written expression, which are different from students whose vision requires the use of assistive technology.

Collaborative teams who have data-informed conversations can create accommodations and, when necessary, modifications that allow them to create IEPs that are individually based on the specific student's strengths and areas of challenge. These teams hold high expectations for student learning at the forefront of the discussion and focus their plans around intentionally creating environments for the student to demonstrate their knowledge and skills. Any supports deemed necessary are those that are based on accurate data with areas to provide teaching strategies to the student to transfer ownership of learning to the student. Collaborative teams work to provide accommodations and modifications consistently throughout the student's school day and collect data throughout the year on the need for the supports as well as when the student demonstrates the need for the team to come back together and restructure the supports based on new skills.

The accommodations checklist example in figure 7.1 can serve as a guide for teams to use in determining what supports the student is currently using in different settings as well as for documentation of the supports for fidelity. We recommend teams use some type of data collection tool for any accommodations or modifications that are included in a student's IEP to inform the continued use of the support and to identify any areas where the team needs to consider a different plan based on the student's current skills.

Accommodations Examples	Daily	Weekly	Monthly	Student implemented	Teacher directed	Notes
Extra Time	X (on assignments)			X		Student uses extra time when completing written work
Asking for a break		X		X		Student asks for a break about once a week after recess
Read aloud of tests						Student often refuses when offered

Figure 7.1: Accommodations checklist.

Conclusion

Accommodations and modifications can be a slippery slope within the classrooms when they aren't supported through data and with a collaborative team understanding of why we have the accommodation and who is responsible for implementing and collecting data around the use of the support. While the right accommodations are necessary for student success, the team supporting the student has to be able to implement the support. Next, we will discuss service minutes and educational placement for students.

Chapter 7 Reflection

Does your team use a structure for providing accommodations or modifications? How are the data supporting the recommendations?

Red Light Areas Identify practices that must stop	**Yellow Light Areas** Identify essential actions to take	**Green Light Areas** Identify actions to continue

CHAPTER 8

DETERMINING SERVICE MINUTES AND PLACEMENT

Over, under, around or through. Find a way or make a way.
—Paula Kluth

Just about anyone who has been on a road trip has heard the question, "Are we there yet?" As with trying to time out how long it will take to reach your destination, trying to determine the number of minutes and placement a student will need to receive their specially designed instruction can be an overwhelming process. Teams may approach service minutes through a variety of methods; some may go off of time blocks (thirty minutes, forty-five minutes, or sixty minutes) or the bell-to-bell schedule. Others may review the curricular tool they are implementing and make recommendations for minutes off of the amount of time to implement the program while other teams approach scheduling minutes based on the planned instruction aligned with the student's specific goal.

IDEA section 300.114 (U.S. Department of Education, 2017c) requires having procedures in place to meet the requirements of the least restrictive environment for all students to participate "to the maximum extent appropriate" with students who are nondisabled. It further tells us that special classrooms, separate schools, and removing students with disabilities from regular education should only occur due to the "severity of the disability" being so extreme that participation in regular education with support and services can't be successfully implemented. Students with the most significant disabilities consist of less than 2 percent of the special education population in the United States (National Center for Education Statistics, 2021). These students qualify for alternate assessments due to their significant cognitive abilities. Also, this same 2 percent of the special education population meets the requirement for the state alternate assessment with many states adopting to use a common assessment, the Dynamic Learning Maps, allowing some congruency across state lines (National Center for Education Statistics, 2021).

When we consider removing students from their guaranteed and viable grade-level general education curriculum, this is the small percentage of students whom we are referring to. These are all the students about whom we say, "yes and," in regard to their service minutes. Otherwise, when teams are removing students from their general education classroom and curriculum, we have to ask why. The harsh and often unfortunate reality around the recommendation of service minutes is that teams recommend minutes that fit within their schedule or programming rather than determining the service minutes that are necessary to support students' IEP goals. Teams will propose 30/45/60 daily minutes or 150/225/300 weekly minutes of service for students. When you ask teams to explain how they determine the minutes they recommend, it often comes down to scheduling for either the special education teachers or the master schedule. We challenge teams to be different and make recommendations that are based on the specially designed instruction they plan to provide.

Connecting Least Restrictive Environment and Service Minutes

When we consider the least restrictive environment, we must start with general education first. We know that teams often say they start in general education first and demonstrate this by having a general education teacher as the teacher of record or the student having a seat in the general education class. But we want you to truly consider *how* you can provide specially designed instruction within the general education setting when you think about the least restrictive environment. When teams look at the IEP goal and then determine how they are going to provide the instruction necessary to meet that goal, they need to determine how much time per day, week, or month they need solely to work on each specific goal. Once they determine the actual goal and their intentional planning of instruction, then they can begin to consider how it aligns with the general education curriculum and determine how much time is necessary for instruction.

Once teams have a solid goal and instructional plan developed, determining how many minutes per week or month are necessary for that plan to be delivered becomes more about the individual student than the schedule. Therefore, the teams no longer look to see where they have thirty-minute blocks of time available or where the independent part of the workshop block is scheduled as the only time to schedule students. Since educators must ensure they are planning for how they will provide services for students in the least restrictive environment, this starts with not just assuming the student is receiving general education instruction but how they are intentionally partnering with the general education teacher to ensure access to the core instruction in their classroom. This access includes how they will provide specially designed instruction that targets the core curriculum and grade-level standards. When educators intentionally partner to take collective ownership of the student's learning, they offer the student a much broader educational experience that empowers both the general education teacher and the special education teacher to truly meet the individual needs of the student. Teams that honestly consider the least restrictive environment first and how they are going to meet the student's needs within the general education classroom create learning environments that allow *all* students to thrive and make progress on their own educational journey.

This proposal of teams collaborating on the strategies they will be implementing and then making a recommendation for how much time these minutes would encompass could be a radical shift for some schools and teams used to only being able to service students during flex time or independent blocks, which results in many students having the same 150 minutes of service regardless of what their needs demonstrate. Teams may feel that going outside of their typical service minute provisions may seem impossible or a scheduling nightmare that is unable to be legally met. We challenge that and ask teams to take a week's worth of data of how much time they are genuinely providing specially designed instruction that is specifically targeting the student's goal. When the week is up, review the times and determine how much time they were providing goal instruction compared to how much time was spent on transitions to or from a separate location, completing warm-up activities or some monitored independent practice, taking a break, or getting help on an assignment or supervised homework help.

Likewise, when educators implement alternative curricular tools as one-size-fits-all solutions, then special education minutes are tied to the program's fidelity rather than the parts of the program necessary for individual students to have their IEP goals addressed. When an alternative curricular tool needs to be implemented, teams need to go through a set of steps (we will go into some options for this in chapter 9, page 101) to ensure they have selected the correct tool and how they will be connecting this tool to the guaranteed and viable curriculum that is in place for the student's grade level.

Service minutes have become one of the least individualized parts of students' IEPs due to teams not having the knowledge or ability to make recommendations based on the student, rather than the schedule. During our times in schools, when we ask a team to provide additional details about what they will be doing with the IEP minutes, typically, they share broad statements about reinforcing skills and building new skills or when the student *must* receive services outside of their classroom due to their ability to attend to the instruction. Seems legit, right? We disagree.

Students spend the other five hours of the school day expected to learn and maintain their progress within an environment that is reportedly so distracting they must be removed from that setting to learn with the special education teacher. If it is necessary for the student to be removed from their typical learning environment for thirty minutes a day with special education, what about the rest of their day? When a student is removed from their grade-level learning environment for any amount of time, teams have to consider how the student accesses learning throughout the remainder of the day and ensure they are teaching strategies that can be generalized to allow the student to be successful across the entire school day.

Another area to consider is identifying how teachers are working collaboratively with the team to support the student while they are in the general education setting and what intentional instructional strategies are planned to teach the student to create a more successful learning environment with the larger group. Teams need to be able to answer the question, "What specifically do we need to teach the student to build into their toolbox and be successful in the larger environment, and what skill is missing that is preventing them from being able to learn and demonstrate their knowledge across all areas of the school?"

Determining the Best Location for Services

Once teams have determined their goal, instructional plan, and service minutes, then they need to determine the best location to deliver these services, starting within the general education setting. If a student *must* receive services outside of their general education setting, the team needs to ensure the instruction delivered aligns with the general education setting, there is a clearly defined plan for how the student will transfer these skills to their classroom, and the team knows how it will support the generalization of these skills across settings. These considerations especially apply to related services where students often go to speech therapy, an occupational therapist, or counseling one or two times a week.

When educators only work on these skills in isolation and in a separate setting, they don't always teach students how to carry these skills with them outside of their classes. Collaboration across the team helps reinforce these skills everywhere. Consider if you want to learn how to cook better and you go to a cooking class once a week. When you get to the cooking class, everything is set up for the cooking activity. However, when you go home, you may think about trying to make that meal again, but you have to figure out all the ingredients and kitchen tools you used as well as the recipe steps. It's no wonder we may become frustrated when our meal doesn't taste as good as it did during a class where the instructor carried the entire cognitive load of that lesson. We want to create an environment where students learn how to generalize what they learn in their daily lives.

Teachers need to ensure they have an intentional plan for the strategies they are teaching students to be generalized and transferred throughout their day, not just to one successful place within the school. When a student struggles in a larger environment and teachers remove that environment but don't teach the student how to use their strategies to be successful, they aren't helping; they are hindering their student's access to the world. When teachers only provide services in a small or even one-on-one environment, it may be easier for them, but it is detrimental to long-term student success.

On the continuum of special education services, each student has their own blend of services, based on their needs, which is fluid. All students can possess a jagged learning profile where they have individual strengths and weaknesses within their skills. Teams need to consider these as they are considering the continuum of services for students. The continuum of special education services ranges from 100 percent general education with no services or support through full residential programming needs. While most students receive their special education services within their neighborhood school, teams always have to examine the student's progress to determine when they can move along that continuum toward success in the general education environment. The student's instructional planning team should be able to access the full continuum for each instructional activity of the student's day when they are designing the student's education, always beginning with general education first (figure 8.1).

	Grade-level classroom	Special 1	Special 2	Common areas	Sped setting	Related service setting	Other
Reading sight words	20 minutes	10 minutes in PE	10 minutes in library				
Using coping strategies	10 minutes	10 minutes in art				10 minutes in group with counseling 10 minutes in speech	5 minutes on the bus
Producing /th/	10 minutes					10 minutes in speech three times a week	

Figure 8.1: Collaborative goal instruction.

In figure 8.2, we have the continuum spread out to demonstrate that it is not necessarily about checking a box for the student's education placement. Teams need to look across the continuum for where services can be provided to meet the educational needs instead of looking at the boxes as a placeholder for the student. We can and should be flexible in our design based on the current reality of the student's strengths and growth areas and where the most appropriate setting is to deliver the specially designed instruction for this student.

General Education	20 percent	40 percent	60 percent	80 percent	100 percent	Therapeutic Day School	Residential or Hospitalization

Figure 8.2: Continuum chart.

School districts and teams can always review their service delivery and review a few key concepts such as the following.

- Where do they provide special education services?
- How are they determining these minutes?
- How are they planning for generalization for any time out of the general education classroom?
- How are they planning collaboratively with the grade-level teacher?
- Is the team progress monitoring to ensure team members are intentionally closing the gap and not allowing the gap to get larger?

Teams can and should explain what it looks like for the students when they are within their grade-level general education classroom. Is the student engaged in the work and carrying the cognitive load? Or are they at a table in the back to allow this time to count toward their general education percentage without generating any learning?

The final area where teams can compare their service delivery is by looking at the breakdowns of services provided to students across the continuum. Are all students in the same minute boxes? Are the service minutes individualized for students? Does everyone receive thirty minutes? Looking at the service delivery breakdown, such as figure 8.2 (page 97), can be the first step in identifying if teams are planning for the individual student or if they are planning for time allotments. In the example in figure 8.3, if you charted out across the continuum, you would notice that almost every student receives services in the 80 percent or above category, even though they have different needs. That could be a sign of quality instructional strategies, or it could be a sign that we are not looking at students' needs individually and having similar minutes for all students. Figure 8.4 can be used to help you chart your students' progress.

Grade Bands	Needs	Service Minutes
K–1	Six students	80 percent or more in general education (six)
2–3	Eight students	80 percent or more in general education (eight)
4–5	Eleven students	80 percent or more in general education (ten)
		Less than 40 percent in general education (one)

Figure 8.3: Program review.

	100 percent general education	80 percent general education	40 to 79 percent general education	Less than 40 percent general education	100 percent special education	Outplacement
Number of students in each						
Number of students with goals aligned to grade level						
Number of students showing improvement on both goals and district assessment						
If less than 60 percent of time in general education, number of students with independence goal						
Students have meaningful and intentional engagement within general education						
Students participate in grade-level specials classes and lunch (art, PE, music, field trips, and so on)						

Figure 8.4: Program review of students' progress.

Visit **go.SolutionTree.com/specialneeds** *to download a free reproducible version of this figure.*

Conclusion

As part of a collaborative team, identifying how much time is needed for target instruction toward a goal is crucial in ensuring that the individual student's needs are met in their least restrictive environment. Your service minutes and placement recommendations are just as important as in the previous sections. These cannot be accomplished without a collaborative team effort to determine how much time each person is going to provide instruction toward the goal area and where that instruction best takes place, leading to all the team members having the collective responsibility for the student's growth toward their goals.

In chapter 9, we will look at some of the less common areas special education teams face such as behavior plans, assistive technology, and supporting low-incidence populations. Each of these areas is a vital support for the specific students who require them. In this, we will only look at a brief overview of the areas.

Chapter 8 Reflection

How do your teams determine service minutes and student placement?

Red Light Areas	**Yellow Light Areas**	**Green Light Areas**
Identify practices that must stop	Identify essential actions to take	Identify actions to continue

CHAPTER 9

EXPLORING BEHAVIOR, ASSISTIVE TECH, TRANSITION, AND LOW INCIDENCE

Every child can learn, just not always on the same day or in the same way.

—George Evans

The field of special education is a multifaceted adventure where each view could take you on an entirely different adventure. When we began to craft this book, we wanted it to serve as a tool for teams and families to use in building stronger IEPs for students to ensure they have the same guaranteed access to high learning outcomes as their peers. As we sketched out our approach to each chapter, we became acutely aware of the many ways each topic could result in incomprehensibly lengthy chapters. Frankly, we could devote multiple books to any of the topics, given the due diligence they require. In this chapter, we will briefly cover a few additional areas of special education services, such as behavior, assistive technology, low incidence and related services, and transition. However, you should consider this information an initial primer only, as a comprehensive understanding of these areas needs a deeper dive into the world of special education to fully embrace their concepts.

Behavior

The collective understanding of how behavior impacts performance within schools has been evolving since the late 1990s. Schools started examining behavior as we came to understand more about autism and mental health, especially after many schools worked to respond to the inclusion approaches in the 1990s. Likewise, when restorative justice practices began to rise in schools, our behavior journey continued, and we tried to understand the rationale behind the behaviors (Center for Urban Education Success, n.d.). As students become increasingly active participants within their general education schools, educator teams recognized the need to understand how to support students struggling with consistently demonstrating expected behaviors across the day. One of the trickiest parts of supporting behavior is understanding and accepting the concept that all forms of behavior are a form of communication (Pacer Center, 2020). We may not like how it's being communicated or even understand what is being communicated, but the behavior is always communication.

Once we accept that behavior is communicating something to us, frustration, anxiety, hunger, or even just a sense of being overwhelmed, the next step is accepting that the adult is not the true target of this behavior, and it is not an intentional personal attack. Behaviorists have long established that behavior stems from the need for escape, attention, tangible items, or sensory needs (Lovering, 2023). None of these are bad behaviors or a demonstration of a student being "naughty" (Iris Center, n.d.). The important part is to identify which need the student is communicating through their behavior that something is not OK, and we need to implement support.

No matter the underlying reason for challenging behavior—be it related to a mental health diagnosis, autism, ADHD, or going through a really difficult time—school teams must ensure they are supporting the student through the lens of positive connections and data. School teams can conduct a functional behavior analysis (FBA) to build a collective understanding of what is driving the behavior, where it is occurring, and what strategies are working to help develop a set of proactive strategies and steps to support the student as well as identify what skills need to be taught. When teams determine an FBA is necessary, specific times and behaviors are examined by the team to determine if a common behavior can be identified, as well as examine what happened right before and right after the behavior to help establish what is supporting the behavior as well as what is precipitating the behavior.

Data collection around behavior can be one of the more challenging pieces where teams may need to problem solve on what the best method is, number of occurrences, time intervals, or duration. In collecting any sort of data, teams should ensure the data collection is not only consistent across stakeholders but also collecting relevant information that can inform how the student is making progress. For example, if a student is refusing to engage in a task, taking data across stakeholders will be key to ensure we are documenting appropriately, including prompts, type of prompts, type of response, and timing. If one person is only documenting what the student does but not what the adults are doing, we are missing part of the data puzzle. There is no one-size-fits-all approach to working through behavior challenges, as they require a personalized approach for the student and the team.

Assistive Technology

Assistive technology is one of the most fascinating fields within special education and all of education right now. The huge technological advances in generative artificial intelligence (AI; such as ChatGPT) have opened the doors to how we can support all students with more and more technologies readily available and accessible to everyone. As AI continues to advance, it may become commonplace across the educational environment and move us forward with a universal design for the learning model and require less assistive technology as dedicated resources. For example, many students have access to programs that auto-generate text such as Grammarly (https://app.grammarly.com); previously this may have been considered to be assistive technology for the predictive text features for students who struggle with writing. Under IDEA, assistive technology is a service students access to assist with the "selection, acquisition, or use of an assistive technology device" (U.S. Department of Education, 2019a). Assistive technology services include the following.

- Evaluation
- Purchase or lease of a device
- Design, fit, customize, and adapt the device or tool
- Maintain, repair, and replace a device
- Coordinate with other services
- Train and provide technical assistance for the student, family, and teams (school and home)

Often, when we think of the assistive technology team, we primarily think of nonverbal students using augmentative and alternative communication (AAC) devices. While this plays a huge part in the field of assistive technology, there are many more areas in which assistive technology can provide support to teams. Assistive technology can be considered for writing and language support as well as for executive functioning skills. Individuals who have physical disabilities can also benefit from assistive technology services. Some examples of assistive technology could be something as simple as speech-to-text or spellcheck software or more complex tools such as a touch button or switch or eye-blink reader. Often, students may use predictive text to help them find words when they are writing or apps that allow them to keep everything in one electronic source (such as a digital notebook like Notability [https://notability.com] or Microsoft OneNote [www.onenote.com]).

What makes an assistive technology evaluation slightly different from other types of evaluations is its design. While other specialty areas can rely on standardized assessments and formalized tools, an assistive technology evaluation revolves around identified areas of concern being addressed through team collaboration, problem solving, trialing of tools, and data collection. For an assistive technology evaluation to be successful, the team must function at the highest collaboration levels, understanding their strength as a collective group of individuals coming together to determine possible options for the student. There are some formal training aspects involved within the field of assistive technology. However, there are not always dedicated assistive technology teams available to districts, leading to school teams utilizing their resources to evaluate tools. Collaborative teams look at the strengths of the student and identify areas where the student could use these strengths. Next, they review the IEP goals that may need support through assistive technology. Then, the team collaborates on what additional tools and strategies should be used and how they could be implemented in the classroom setting. These tools may be software programs such as Learning Ally (https://learningally.org) or Google Docs (www.google.com/docs) to complete assignments. Finally, teams begin the implementation stage and introduce the assistive technology device to the student who begins to use the tool while the teams collect data on the progress. During this trial period, teams engage in regular meetings to determine if the tool is working, how the implementation is going, and analyze if the data demonstrate the expected improvement. At the end of the trial period, teams must come back together to review the results and make a final recommendation.

For teams and districts, assistive technology can have some tricky areas. The first being in determining what is assistive technology and what is an accommodation. In some districts, all students have access to specific technology tools that other districts might consider to be assistive technology tools, such as premium Read&Write for Google Chrome (www.texthelp.com) or access to audiobooks. With technology programs advancing, some districts have access to these for all students as part of their core curriculum. In these cases, as well as when a formalized assistive technology evaluation is necessary, teams must ensure they are problem solving through a data-informed lens and documenting within the IEP if the student requires this to be successful, even if the tool is offered to all students.

The second tricky area for completing assistive technology evaluations is understanding who can or should complete the evaluation. In serving the individual student's needs, it is key to include an assistive technology evaluator who understands the student's disability as well as has in-depth knowledge of the area the team is looking for support. The same individual who specializes in AAC device usage may not be the best option for a student who struggles with written expression output unless they are cross-trained and have had the opportunity to build expertise with written expression as well. The tools that support assistive technology continue to evolve, and new ones develop, so collaborative teams need to reach out to their districts, agencies, organizations, and so on if they need support in assistive technology as they cannot be experts in all areas.

Low-Incidence Disabilities

The U.S. Department of Education (2019b) considers *low-incidence disabilities* to be those that are visual, hearing, or significant cognitive impairments, or impairments where few staff have the highly specialized skills and knowledge to be able to provide services. In the field of special education, disabilities that are considered low incidence have teams working as singletons or outliers with the rest of the school and even special education teams. These teams often support some of our most complex learners and require the most extensive alternative planning. As we discussed in chapter 2, Friziellie and colleagues (2016) share a planning format (figure 2.1, page 30) for answering the question, "Do we expect this student to function independently in life?" If yes, we stay at grade-level expectations. If not, we consider an alternative personalized progression through standards.

Due to the impact of their disability, many students within low-incidence populations are not expected to function independently in adulthood. However, not every student who is considered to be low incidence within their school district is an automatic *no*, nor does it mean the student must always have a completely alternative curriculum. In addition, are there areas where teams can build more independence? Teams continue to operate as a *yes* until they have concrete evidence that the answer is *no* for this student. Until there is any doubt, stay with *yes* and maintain grade-level standards.

Some disabilities, such as a significant visual or hearing impairment, may be considered district-based, low-incidence disabilities. With the right support, many students with disabilities can live independently (Impact on Life, n.d.). Teams need to ensure they are working with teachers who are trained to work with deaf students or those who have a visual or hearing impairment to appropriately plan to ensure grade-level access to the general education curriculum while meeting the individual needs of the student. Often, teachers who are deaf or have a hearing impairment, hard of hearing, or visual impairment only focus on their specialty areas and show a high degree of focus on advocacy. However, we need to ensure these specialists are active team members and are part of planning academics and grade-level instruction for the students. These teams must be collaborative and share specific strategies for ensuring access to the grade-level content and how the student can demonstrate their knowledge.

When teams plan for a student's individual standards, which may align with alternative standards, teams focus more on team-based goals and maximizing the strengths of each student. These team planning opportunities also have a high degree of focus on independence as well as person-centered planning, by looking at goal areas and building these together to determine where the focus on skills can be shared among the entire team.

When considering the person-centered planning approach, teams focus on the individual goals and the student's strengths. They determine how to build on these for the next year with the most important skills or areas that align with the family's goals. It is an opportunity to dream big and discuss what a successful school year looks like and what a successful home year looks like from the family's viewpoint. When school and home teams have open, collaborative conversations about what is most important, teams can support one another through instruction and by sharing skill concepts.

Teams often look at alternative, sometimes boxed, curriculum sets for a set scope and sequence when supporting a student whose needs align with the alternative standards. As we have discussed previously, we would challenge that while boxed curricular tools *can* be a great and valuable resource, each student must have their own guaranteed and viable curriculum based on who they are as a learner, their specific strengths, their specific challenges, and how their levels of independence are impacted. When we only use one tool across an entire classroom or one method, we are limited in what we can expect for individual progress.

If a team is looking for a specific tool to implement, we would encourage team members to engage in problem solving with the student's IEP team to look for ways in which everyone's lens of expertise is able to examine the tool and how they can support the student and help with supporting strategies. The team also needs to consider the student's IEP goals, how this tool supports the IEP goal area through specialized instruction, and what the next step would be after this goal is complete. In many cases, when we quickly choose a tool because it fits current needs, we don't consider how this bridges back to the general education or grade-level standard rather than only supporting a parallel delivery where the specially designed instruction does not align with the general education curriculum and a student experiences parallel instruction.

When we have cross-categorical, self-contained classrooms supporting our most complex learners, teams must ensure that we are continuing to look at each student as an individual, on a specific grade level, not a *program name* student. A pitfall can be when districts run a program model, such as life skills, structure, or behavior as the common features, leading our thought process to only see these specific areas and only focus on these areas. As teams collaborate and build systems of support across the school settings, we must continue to plan for the individual student's areas of needs and not plan for the wide range of needs across the cohort of students. Teams need to consider a few more things to ensure they are providing access to the least restrictive environment and grade-level peers at every opportunity, ensuring students participate in their grade-level specials, lunch, recess, field trips, and general education classes.

Related Services Within Low Incidence

The scheduling for service providers to support students identified with additional needs within the school can be one of life's greatest challenges. Typically, right when you think you finally have it, either a student moves in or out, or a teacher has to change their schedule based on a different external factor. Scheduling for teams supporting students with complex needs can be challenging, especially if teams generally consider pushing in or co-serving within a self-contained classroom as the most viable option, which can sometimes offer the most flexibility. However, is this type of classroom the best option for the individual student's progress? When we start to schedule students within the same classroom for all specials and related services together, we lose the aspect of having other peers, or other peers with different needs, as models. When considering your schedules as related service team members, teams need to consider that when serving students across grade levels together, are we creating separate AAC groups or social groups for the grade level that allow for different peers to come together? For adaptive physical education, are we having a PE class for the entire self-contained class, or are we serving adapted PE minutes during their grade-level PE, or do we have an assigned time to allow the teacher to have a plan?

Transition Services

In 1983, IDEA began to implement official *transition services* for students, services that act as a "coordinated set of activities" focused on both academics and functional services for school to postsecondary education, vocational services, and integrated supported employment, independent living, and community engagement (U.S. Department of Education, 2017b). Transition services focus on the student's individual needs, strengths, and interests and can be supported through instruction, related services, and community experiences. These services also may focus on areas of daily living for the individual student.

In most U.S. states, this planning starts at age 16, but it can start earlier and can continue through age 21. Several states start the transition planning for the child around 14½ years or at the end of middle or junior high school so that the high school teams have a direction of where the student and family are planning for life after high school. Serving students within transition programs is done by a specialized team of individuals focusing on transition skills, including vocational, job skills, and life skills, that blend between the high school setting and adult life. These teams may be comprised of special education teachers, related service personnel, job coaches, vocational coaches, and supportive employment staff.

This team focuses on building bridges into adulthood with a highly specialized focus on increasing independence, activities of daily living, vocational training, and job skills based on the student's strengths and interests. Transition teams approach each student through a unique lens of their abilities, hopes, and dreams, and facilitate the family planning for a post-secondary transition. Teams spend time working through the complexities of supported employment, supported living, discovering recreational and leisure activities, and finding avenues to embed structures for independence.

Transition teams build on their collaborative practices, skills, and strategies that not only complement one another but offer a generalization to other areas as students need to take what they are learning and be able to apply these same skills and strategies throughout their lives. During collaboration meetings, teams must focus on their strategies, examine data, and build layers of independence for their students. The degree of student specialization that occurs within transition is extremely high, and these teams have to engage in collaborative planning to meet the individual student needs from a team approach. The entire focus on transition should be to get the student as independent as possible.

Conclusion

Behavior, assistive technology, low-incidence disabilities, and transition services all deserve to have the same level of intensity of support within school communities. From a collaborative team lens, everyone needs to have professional practice thought partners, even if they feel like a singleton within their school districts. Across the United States, many teams support our most complex learners in all types of educational environments. If you are supporting a student and want to reach out to others to be thought partners or collaborative problem solvers, reach out to your school or district administration to help connect you with others who have similar caseloads. If you need help reaching out beyond your district, district administration can reach out to either of us, and we are happy to help connect you with others who may be singletons looking for collaborative partners as well. Supporting students with special education needs is our passion, and we hope that you have found in this book the tools to help on your students' journey.

Chapter 9 Reflection

When it comes to the additional topics of assistive technology, behavior intervention plans, and low-incidence special education, where are you as school or district teams?

Red Light Areas	Yellow Light Areas	Green Light Areas
Identify practices that must stop	Identify essential actions to take	Identify actions to continue

Epilogue

*You did what you knew how to do, and
when you knew better, you did better.*

—Maya Angelou

Our road trip through meaningful, life-changing IEP writing has almost reached its destination. As the great Maya Angelou leads, now that we know better, we have to do better. Our roles as educators and members of a student's IEP team are ones that allow us the opportunity to change the lives of the students we encounter. When we approach that responsibility with the level of care and intentionality it rightly deserves, we are able to harness our collective knowledge for the benefit of our students. The success of students who receive services depends not only on what the special education teacher does, but also on what the classroom, grade-, or content-level teacher is doing, what the family is doing, and how we are all working together to support the student. Our friends at Lead Inclusion often share great thoughts about the success of inclusion and inclusive practices such as, "When special educators become inclusion specialists who collaborate on instruction with UDL, there will be less specially designed instruction needed for individual students" (Jung, 2023). The powers of working together as collaborative teams help both general education and special education teachers to be better equipped to support the learning and growth of all students. Acknowledging that we are active members of collaborative teams, we tie ourselves to the concepts of continual improvement, knowing that we grow together as a team through every conversation, strategy implementation, and data collection opportunity. As special education teams, it is essential that we embrace continual improvement for ourselves and our students to create a better world each day. Leading the shift within special education can be an uphill mountain climb that may feel like Mount Everest some days, forcing us to shift not only our own mindsets but also the mindsets of multiple teams, perhaps even entire schools or districts. Sometimes, it means even shifting the mindsets of parents or guardians. Ultimately, this shifting of stakeholders' mindsets is what is required for life-changing special education.

We hope you will use the concepts in this book to examine how teams are supporting students, both those with IEPs and those who may be struggling learners looking for a team to wrap around them with intentional strategies. While we love to go out and enjoy a good road trip, we want you to be able to have the strategies and skills to build your road trip adventure. Through the examples, reproducibles, appendices, and reflection stoplights, we challenge you to have open conversations, identify your current baselines, and build out your progressions, while also planning for pit stops, possible detours, and road construction as you journey toward providing life-changing special education.

Now that we have arrived at our current destination, we will always seek to build out our next adventure through collaboration, data collection, problem solving, and failing forward. With each time our GPS announces it's "recalculating," we know that we will have the opportunity to grow our skills, learn new things, and build into one another. Our journey to life-changing special education will never stop or be truly complete because each adventure will give us new skills, new opportunities, and new advancements in education. We hope you enjoyed the adventure and long-lived road trips. We truly have had the time of our lives!

APPENDIX A

Examples of PLAAFPs and Goals

This appendix provides examples of PLAAFPs and goals to guide you as your team creates present levels and goal areas. These are not meant to be full examples or perfect options. They are here to give you some perspectives on how a PLAAFP or an annual goal could look for a student.

Keep in mind, the goals align to a grade-level priority standard and are based on the impact of the student's disability. The example goals align toward specific present levels and ensure the four checks (page 70) are met.

Early Childhood

In an early childhood classroom, often the focus is on school readiness skills, such as following routines, emerging academic and functional skills, as well as communication, fine motor, and problem solving. Samantha, our hypothetical emerging kindergarten student, has been working hard on following expectations and transitioning throughout the classroom.

PLAAFP

Samantha enjoys painting and playing in the blocks station. She does a great job in building towers that are four to five blocks high.

Samantha is learning the classroom routines and structures as a rising four-year-old. She is beginning to be able to follow one-step oral directions. However, she can become distracted by preferred play areas or people. Samantha is not yet engaging verbally in conversations with peers, but she is observant and appears to be listening to them during conversations and play. She enjoys watching her peers during dramatic play and becomes very excited when her peers are excited.

Samantha does not yet ask for help when she needs something and will instead either move on to something else or become frustrated. In play stations, if she can't figure out a toy, she will move on to a different activity. In play, Samantha will play alongside a peer but does not yet engage in reciprocal play with peers or adults. She will tell a peer or adult "no" if they try to take her toy or if she does not want to do something.

Samantha will sort items into two colors when working on early math skills. She is not yet able to sort by size or shape. Samantha is able to demonstrate "1" when working in a one-on-one setting, handing one piece or object for "give me 1." She is able to identify "blue." When asked for the "blue block," she will point to or hand the blue object. She is inconsistent in identifying red, yellow, or green. For her early reading skills, Samantha follows along when being read to and will pick up a book, holding it correctly. Samantha will often flip through pages of the book and get to preferred pictures. Samantha does not yet answer questions about a book or the pictures she sees in the books.

Goal

By the next annual review, when in a play area (within the school or the playground), Samantha will engage in reciprocal play with a peer with a minimum of five toys, objects, or exchanges with the peer in four out of five charted opportunities.

So What?: *This goal is important for Samantha to be able to engage in play with peers to build on her ability to participate in groups, games, and partner work.*

Stranger: *The goal clearly states what Samantha needs to be able to demonstrate (five exchanges with a peer) and in any location at school (classroom or playground).*

Lunchbox: *These steps are written as positive actions we want Samantha to demonstrate with a peer.*

Life-Changing: *Samantha will have other peers in her educational life and needs to be able to take turns, share, and engage with other peers in a play setting.*

Early Elementary

Early elementary students (typically through second grade) are learning the basic foundations of reading, writing, and mathematics. They are learning new skills at a rapid pace, going from barely identifying letters and sounds at the beginning of their kindergarten year to reading at winter break. The focus is on helping Mateo bridge from individual sounds to blending sounds together to make a word, which for this hypothetical second grader, would have been well established by this point in their education.

PLAAFP

Mateo has strong knowledge of print, holds the book correctly, enjoys flipping through pages, and identifies pictures and sight words. Mateo knows all twenty-six uppercase and lowercase letters both expressively and receptively. Mateo can identify twenty of the first 100 Fry sight words in isolation and in print. Mateo can identify sounds for all letters and is working on blends. Mateo is able to identify the first and last sounds in isolation and is approximately 50 percent accurate in identifying medial sounds in consonant, vowel, consonant (CVC) words. Mateo does not yet blend sounds in CVC or consonant, vowel, vowel, consonant (CVVC) words. In the winter, using Northwest Evaluation Association (NWEA) Measures of Academic Progress (MAP assessment), Mateo achieved a RIT score of 150, which placed him in the first percentile. This score means that Mateo scored at or better than 1 percent of students nationally who participated in the winter assessment. Mateo's strengths were basic reading and literature.

Goal

By the next annual review, when presented with a CVVC word, Mateo will use his reading skills to decode the word with 90 percent accuracy in four out of five charted opportunities.

So What?: *This goal is important for Mateo to grow in his reading skills and decode unfamiliar words, making him a more fluent reader.*

Stranger: *The goal clearly states what Mateo needs to complete to meet the goal. He must have CVVC words, know what those are, and decode the entire word with 90 percent accuracy.*

Lunchbox: *These steps are written in positive actions we want Mateo to complete to improve his reading fluency.*

Life-Changing: *Mateo gaining the skills to decode words and read words that are unfamiliar will provide him with access to higher-level text and increase his ability to read fluently.*

Late Elementary

In late elementary (third through fifth grade), students move toward building on those foundational basic reading and mathematics skills. Tenley has not yet been able to demonstrate a solid understanding of complex multiplication and division problems. As someone who is ending her fifth-grade year and moving into sixth grade, this skill is necessary for her to focus on and solve independently.

PLAAFP

Tenley has great knowledge of addition and subtraction and can solve three-digit by three-digit addition and subtraction problems independently. She is inconsistent in her ability to demonstrate learning of two-digit by one-digit multiplication and division problems. Tenley is able to recite her math facts of multiplication by 0 and by 1. When grouping, she can make equal groups; however, she has not been able to transfer this skill to division.

Tenley demonstrates an understanding of the place values of ones, tens, and hundreds. In working with fractions, she can demonstrate $\frac{1}{2}$, $\frac{1}{4}$, and $\frac{1}{3}$. She is inconsistent in her ability to build fractions to create a whole ($\frac{1}{2} + \frac{1}{4} + \frac{1}{4} = 1$).

Tenley's most recent NWEA MAP scores are the following.

Winter 2024: 178 or 10 percentile

Fall 2023: 177 or 14 percentile

Spring 2023: 177 or 30 percentile

Winter 2023: 172 or 25 percentile

Goal

By the annual review, when presented with a word problem that requires the use of four-digit by three-digit multiplication or division, Tenley will choose the correct operation and solve the problem with 80 percent accuracy in four out of five charted opportunities.

So What?: *Solving multistep math problems is a foundational skill that will provide deeper levels of math learning later in life.*

Stranger: *The goal clearly states which operations are measured, the level of accuracy, and what the conditions are for solving (four-digit by three-digit numbers).*

Lunchbox: *This goal shows what Tenley will be able to do for her math skills.*

Life-Changing: *Students must be able to solve multistep math problems across a variety of settings, including math, science, and problem solving.*

Middle School

One of the key pieces of middle school is to help students learn to rely on their own knowledge and skills rather than have a teacher facilitate the learning. Scarlett has difficulty with attending and keeping her thoughts in a coherent structure. By adding a rubric, we are promoting Scarlett's ability to check her work and attend to the details that are necessary for her to complete grade-level expectations.

PLAAFP

Scarlett has many great ideas and thoughts to share verbally. She can elaborate on most given topics and has an extensive knowledge base that she uses to add to her thinking. When having to create structured paragraphs, Scarlett is unable to create coherent paragraphs. Scarlett's sentences can become jumbled or confusing to the reader with multiple topics incorporated, creating run-on sentences, and sentences without subject-verb agreement. Scarlett's use of grammar and punctuation is grade-level appropriate with proper capitalization and punctuation. Scarlett can become frustrated when someone else reads her writing because they are unable to follow the thought pattern and struggle to understand the meaning. Scarlett will inconsistently use prewriting strategies such as thought generators, brainstorming, or graphic organizers. Scarlett will go back and edit her work with prompting. However, she can become frustrated that the paragraph does not read the way she intended, leading her to erase her work and start over.

Goal

By the annual review, when given a topic and provided with technology, graphic organizers, rubrics, and checklists, Scarlett will compose a response to the topic that will include a topic sentence, supporting details, complete sentences, and a closing statement for each response earning a three out of four on the following rubric in four out of five charted opportunities.

Scarlett's Rubric

- My response answers the specific topic.
- My supporting details sentences are complete sentences and are related to the topic.
- My closing sentence is a complete sentence and summarizes my response.
- My sentences all support the same topic.

I used _____ strategy to help me organize my thoughts.

Attach this rubric with checkmarks and any strategy pages with your assignment, please! Great job! You are working hard, Scarlett!

So What?: This goal is important for Scarlett to be able to organize her thoughts and produce a written response to support her opinion.

> ***Stranger:*** *The goal clearly states what steps Scarlett needs to take to accomplish the goal and provides a rubric and checklist for her and anyone monitoring the goal.*
>
> ***Lunchbox:*** *These steps are written as positive actions for Scarlett to take to complete her written response.*
>
> ***Life-Changing:*** *When Scarlett is able to craft a written response to a topic in a clear, coherent manner, she will be able to demonstrate her ability to synthesize information as well as demonstrate her learning.*

High School

High school-aged students focus on goals that are tied to their postsecondary success. In the hypothetical case of Richard, he struggles to organize his time, keep track of his assignments, and then submit the assignments due to the impact of his ADHD.

> ### PLAAFP
>
> *Richard has transitioned nicely to the new building. He is able to navigate all of his classes and knows his way around the building. Richard shared that he felt more comfortable after having been able to tour the building before school opening. While he has an entirely new team this year, he has been growing in his skills to manage multiple assignments and due dates. Richard began using his phone to manage his assignments through calendar invites that he sends to himself or places on his calendar when they are assigned. One area that Richard is still working on is previewing his calendar each week and each day to know what he has coming up and to plan his days accordingly. Richard currently works with his case manager three times a week to prioritize his tasks and schedule when he is going to work on each task, not only when it is due. Richard is also working on appropriately allocating enough time to complete the tasks or activities. He only books ten-minute increments on his calendar because he prefers to see more free time available on his calendar. Richard is approximately 50 percent at turning in his work on time in each course. In about half of the instances, he has completed the work but does not send it to the teacher or online classroom. We have added a nightly check to ensure he turns in all of his completed work each day.*
>
> ### Goal
>
> *By the annual review, to prepare for post-secondary success, Richard will use his resources (technology, checklist, or organizer) to manage his assignments*

and activities and submit completed assigned tasks on time with no more than two adult prompts per week in four out of five charted opportunities.

So What?: This goal is important for self-responsibility and to be able to demonstrate his abilities on the assigned tasks, necessary for postsecondary success.

Stranger: This goal clearly states what Richard needs to do to accomplish the goal and provides options in the event technology needs change or a more successful avenue is established.

Lunchbox: These steps are written using positive actions for Richard to undertake.

Life-Changing: When Richard is able to manage his time and submit completed assignments on time, he will be able to demonstrate his ability to prioritize his assignments, submit them appropriately, and plan his time.

Post–High School Transition

For a student who is learning in a transition program, the focus areas can be individualized based on the strengths of the student. Our hypothetical student Chris has learned to be prompt, but he is dependent on his previous setting, and he will not initiate help if he can't complete his assigned task, hindering his ability to complete work independently on a job site.

PLAAFP

Chris participates well in small groups and familiar environments. Chris depends on his work and communication partner to anticipate his needs and inconsistently advocates for what he is missing or needs to complete an activity or task. When working in a one-on-one or individual setting, Chris can follow his work system and depend on his structures to be aware of how much work he needs to complete and in what order to do so. If Chris runs out of an item or something is incorrect (such as the stapler jamming or missing details about a specific item), Chris will sit and wait for a peer or support person to become aware of this and see that he is not working. If asked what is wrong or if he needs help, Chris will inconsistently respond with what he needs depending on his familiarity with the other individual.

Goal

By the annual review, when completing independent tasks or activities, and having a difficulty or missing item, Chris will initiate help, demonstrate his need to a preferred and less familiar individual, and return to the activity (using a direction to work schedule cue) with no more than three adult prompts in four out of five charted opportunities.

So What?: *This goal is important for adult success.*

Stranger: *This goal clearly states what Chris needs to do to accomplish the goal.*

Lunchbox: *These steps are written using positive actions for Chris to undertake.*

Life-Changing: *When Chris can ask for help and return to work, he is demonstrating greater independence in a variety of work environments providing greater access for him.*

APPENDIX B

Collaborative IEPs: Current Reality, Identifying Essential Actions, and Action Steps

Use this book (especially in a book study) to track your red, yellow, and green light areas.

Red light areas: An opportunity for us to pause and reflect, identify where we are currently, and identify practices we must stop.

Yellow light areas: An opportunity to slow down and determine if we have the right essential actions. In other words, are we moving in the right direction?

Green light areas: An opportunity to move forward in an identified direction.

Red, Yellow, and Green Light Areas

	Red Light Areas Identify practices that must stop	Yellow Light Areas Identify essential actions to take	Green Light Areas Identify actions to continue
Chapter 1: Discovering Why Collaborative IEPs Are Essential			
Chapter 2: Taking a Collaborative Approach			
Chapter 3: Including Parents and Guardians as Partners in the IEP Process			
Chapter 4: Writing the PLAAFP Statement			
Chapter 5: Writing Goals—Getting Started			
Chapter 6: Writing Goals—Data Considerations			
Chapter 7: Understanding Accommodations and Modifications			
Chapter 8: Determining Service Minutes and Placement			
Chapter 9: Exploring Behavior, Assistive Tech, Transition, and Low Inciden			
Epilogue			

The Collaborative IEP © 2025 Solution Tree Press • SolutionTree.com
Visit **go.SolutionTree.com/specialneeds** to download this free reproducible.

References and Resources

American Association of School Administrators. (2022). *IDEA full funding: Hill talking points.* Accessed at www.aasa.org/docs/default-source/advocacy/idea-full-funding-tp-2022.pdf?sfvrsn=2ca82fde_3 on January 2, 2024.

Bailey, K., & Jakicic, C. (2023). *Common formative assessment: A toolkit for Professional Learning Communities at Work* (2nd ed.). Bloomington, IN: Solution Tree Press.

Bailey, K., Jakicic, C., & Spiller, J. (2014). *Collaborating for success with the Common Core: A toolkit for Professional Learning Communities at Work.* Bloomington, IN: Solution Tree Press.

Buffum, A., Mattos, M., & Malone, J. (2018). *Taking action: A handbook for RTI at Work.* Bloomington, IN: Solution Tree Press.

Buffum, A., Mattos, M., & Weber, C. (2009). *Pyramid response to intervention: RTI, professional learning communities, and how to respond when kids don't learn.* Bloomington, IN: Solution Tree Press.

Buffum, A., Mattos, M., & Weber, C. (2012). *Simplifying response to intervention: Four essential guiding principles.* Bloomington, IN: Solution Tree Press.

Center for Urban Education Success. (n.d.). *Restorative practices.* Accessed at www.rochester.edu/warner/cues/restorative-practices on May 20, 2024.

Cornell Law School. (2007). *34 CFR § 300.321 – IEP team.* Accessed at www.law.cornell.edu/cfr/text/34/300.321 on February 29, 2024.

Cornell Law School. (n.d.). *34 CFR § 300.322 – Parent participation.* Accessed at www.law.cornell.edu/cfr/text/34/300.322 on February 29, 2024.

Council for Exceptional Children. (2024). *High-leverage practices for students with disabilities* (2nd ed.). Arlington, VA: Author.

The Council for Persons with Disabilities [@PTBOCPD]. (2021, December 23). *Accessibility is being able to get in the building. Diversity is getting invited to the table. Inclusion is having a* [Image attached] [Post]. X. Accessed at https://x.com/PTBOCPD/status/1474032468005167104?lang=en on September 6, 2024.

DuFour, R., DuFour, R., Eaker, R., Many, T. W., Mattos, M., & Muhammad, A. (2024). *Learning by doing: A handbook for Professional Learning Communities at Work* (4th ed.). Bloomington, IN: Solution Tree Press.

Eaker, R., & Marzano, R. J. (Eds.). (2020). *Professional Learning Communities at Work and High Reliability Schools: Cultures of continuous learning.* Bloomington, IN: Solution Tree Press.

Erkens, C. (2016). *Collaborative common assessments: Teamwork. Instruction. Results.* Bloomington, IN: Solution Tree Press.

Friziellie, H., Schmidt, J. A., & Spiller, J. (2016). *Yes we can! General and special educators collaborating in a professional learning community.* Bloomington, IN: Solution Tree Press.

Goodwin, B. (2022). *Unleashing the power of best first instruction.* Denver, CO: McREL International. Accessed at https://files.eric.ed.gov/fulltext/ED627069.pdf on March 1, 2024.

GovInfo. (1975). *Public Law 94-142—Nov. 29, 1975.* Accessed at www.govinfo.gov/content/pkg/STATUTE-89/pdf/STATUTE-89-Pg773.pdf on January 2, 2024.

Hattie, J. (2011). *Visible learning for teachers: Maximizing impact on learning.* New York, NY: Routledge.

Illinois State Board of Education. (2020, August). *Educational rights and responsibilities: Understanding special education in Illinois.* Accessed at www.isbe.net/Documents/Parent-Guide-Special-Ed-Aug20.pdf on January 2, 2024.

Impact on Life. (n.d.). *Independent living if you are deaf or hearing impaired.* Accessed at www.impactonlife.com/sight-and-hearing-guides/independent-living-hearing-impaired.asp on May 17, 2024.

Individuals With Disabilities Education Improvement Act of 2004, Pub. L. No. 108-446 § 300.115 (2004).Iris Center. (n.d.). *How can Ms. Rollison determine why Joseph behaves the way he does?* Accessed at https://iris.peabody.vanderbilt.edu/module/fba/cresource/q2/p08 on March 7, 2024.

Jung, L. A. (2023). *To the extent that special #educators become #inclusion specialists who collaborate on instruction with #UDL, there will be less specially-designed* [Thumbnail][Post]. LinkedIn. Accessed at www.linkedin.com/posts/lajung_to-the-extent-that-special-educators-activity-7095788589707399170-Lupp on September 5, 2024.

Library of Congress. (1982, June 28). *Board of education of the Hendrick Hudson Central School District, Westchester County et al v Rowley, by her parents, Rowley et ux.* Accessed at https://tile.loc.gov/storage-services/service/ll/usrep/usrep458/usrep458176/usrep458176.pdf on January 2, 2024.

Lovering, N. (2023, December 5). *What are the four functions of behavior?* Accessed at https://psychcentral.com/autism/functionsofbehavioraba on September 6, 2024.

Lynch, M. (2016, October 15). The power of parents: A primer on parental involvement. *The Edvocate.* Accessed at www.theedadvocate.org/power-parents-primer-parental-involvement on May 20, 2024.

Many, T. W., Maffoni, M. J., Sparks, S. K., & Thomas, T. F. (2022). *Energize your teams: Powerful tools for coaching collaborative teams in PLCs at Work.* Bloomington, IN: Solution Tree Press.

Mattos, M., Buffum, A., Malone, J., Cruz, L. F., Dimich, N., & Schuhl, S. (2025). *Taking action: A handbook for RTI at Work* (2nd ed.). Bloomington, IN: Solution Tree Press.

National Center for Education Statistics. (2020). *Students with disabilities.* Accessed at https://nces.ed.gov/programs/coe/pdf/coe_cgg.pdf on January 2, 2024.

National Center for Education Statistics. (2021). *Students with disabilities.* Accessed at https://nces.ed.gov/programs/coe/pdf/2021/cgg_508c.pdf on March 7, 2024.

National Governors Association Center for Best Practices & Council of Chief State School Officers. (2010a). *Common Core State Standards for English language arts and literacy in history/social studies, science, and technical subjects.* Washington, DC: Authors. Accessed at www.corestandards.org/assets/CCSSI_ELA%20Standards.pdf on September 9, 2024.

National Governors Association Center for Best Practices & Council of Chief State School Officers. (2010b). *Common Core State Standards for mathematics.* Washington, DC: Authors. Accessed at www.thecorestandards.org/assets/CCSSI_Math%20Standards.pdf on June 19, 2024.

National School Boards Association. (2019). Data on disabilities: Good news, bad news on graduation rates Accessed at www.nsba.org/ASBJ/2019/April/Graduation-Rates-Students-Disabilities on September 16, 2024.

O'Brien, J., Pearpoint, J., & Kahn, L. (2015). *The PATH & MAPS handbook: Person-centered ways to build community.* Toronto, Ontario, Canada: Inclusion Press.

Pacer Center. (2020). *Tantrums, tears, and tempers: Behavior is communication.* Accessed at www.pacer.org/parent/php/php-c154.pdf on May 15, 2024.

Quote Investigator. (2022, November 30). *You did what you knew how to do, and when you knew better, you did better.* Accessed at https://quoteinvestigator.com/2022/11/30/did-better on September 5, 2024.

Schimmer, T. (2023). *Redefining student accountability: A proactive approach to teaching behavior outside the gradebook.* Bloomington, IN: Solution Tree Press.

Supreme Court of the United States. (2017). *Endrew F., a minor, by and through his parents and next friends, Joseph F. et al. v. Douglas County School District RE-1.* Accessed at www.supremecourt.gov/opinions/16pdf/15-827_0pm1.pdf on January 2, 2024.

U.S. Department of Education. (2017a, December 7). *Questions and answers (Q&A)* on U.S. Supreme court case decision Endrew F. v. Douglas County School District Re-1. Accessed at https://dese.ade.arkansas.gov/Files/20210107121202_qa-endrewcase-12-07-2017.pdf on September 18, 2024.

U.S. Department of Education. (2017b, May 2). *Sec. 300.43 transition services.* Accessed at https://sites.ed.gov/idea/regs/b/a/300.43 on March 7, 2024.

U.S. Department of Education. (2017c, May 3). *Sec. 300.114 LRE requirements.* Accessed at https://sites.ed.gov/idea/regs/b/b/300.114 on February 29, 2024.

U.S. Department of Education. (2017d, November 16). *Sec. 300.324 development, review, and revision of IEP.* Accessed at https://sites.ed.gov/idea/regs/b/d/300.324 on January 2, 2024.

U.S. Department of Education. (2019a, November 7). *Section 1401.* Accessed at https://sites.ed.gov/idea/statute-chapter-33/subchapter-i/1401 on January 2, 2024.

U.S. Department of Education. (2019b, November 7). *Section 1462 (c).* Accessed at https://sites.ed.gov/idea/statute-chapter-33/subchapter-iv/part-b/1462/c on January 2, 2024.

U.S. Department of Education. (n.d.). *State nonfiscal survey of public elementary/ secondary education.* Accessed at https://nces.ed.gov/ccd/stnfis.asp on January 2, 2024.

Williams, K. (2022). *Ruthless equity: Disrupt the status quo and ensure learning for all students.* n.p.: Wish in One Hand Press.

Index

A

academic achievement, xii
    in PLAAFPs, 40, 47, 51–52
    in PLOPs, 75
accessibility, 37
accommodations, 8, 21, 85–91
    assistive technology and, 104
    checklist for, 90–91
    comparing modifications and, 88
    definition of, 85
    independence and, 29–30
    just-in-case approach to, 89–90
    specifying, 86–87
    using data to inform, 88–90
accountability, 17, 18–20, 27, 52
activities of daily living, 107–108
alignment
    for alternative assessments, 30–31
    of goals and standards, 65–67
    of supports and strategies, xii–xiii
alternative assessments, 30–31, 93–94
alternative curriculum and tools, 17
Angelou, Maya, 5, 109
annual reviews, 62
artificial intelligence, 103
assessment
    accommodations and modifications for, 89
    alternative, 30–31, 93–94
    standards and, 6–7

assistive technology, 103–104
augmentative and alternative communication (AAC) devices, 103

B

Bailey, K., 28
baselines, 77–78
behavior, 101–102
behavior goals, 79
belonging, 37
benchmarks, 20, 66, 78–80
Board of Education v. Rowley, 16
body awareness, 68
boxed programs, 17
Buffum, A., 26, 28, 77

C

ChatGPT, 103
classroom routines, 52
collaborative approach, 25–31
    accommodations and modifications and, 88
    low-incidence disabilities and, 106–107
    parents and guardians in, 33–44
    service minutes and, 95–96
    to writing goals, 65–68
Collaborative Common Assessments (Erkens), 28

Common Formative Assessment: A Toolkit for Professional Learning Communities at Work (Bailey & Jakicic), 28

communication

    accommodations and modifications and, 88

    augmentative and alternative, 103

    behavior as, 101–102

compartmentalization, 2

compliance conversations, 73

continuum of services, 19, 97–98

coping skills, 68

Council for Exceptional Children, 26

Council for Persons With Disabilities, 33, 37

COVID-19 pandemic, 6, 35–36

Cruz, L. F., 26, 77

curriculum

    alternative, 17, 106

    priority standards and, 28

    service minutes and, 94–95

D

data

    for accommodations and modifications, 86, 88–90

    on behavior, 102

    collection of around goals, 80

    on functional performance, 52–54

    interventions and, 20–22

    present levels of performance and, 76

    responsiveness based on, 81–82

    service minutes and, 95

    strengths statements based on, 49

    writing goals and, 64, 73–83

De Florio, I., 47

Dimich, N., 26, 77

diversity, 37

DuFour, R., 77

Dynamic Learning Maps, 30–31, 93–94

E

Eaker, R., 28

early childhood goals and PLAAFP examples, 111–112

early elementary goals and PLAAFP examples, 112–113

Education for All Handicapped Children Act, 15

Endrew F. v. Douglas County, 1, 8, 14, 16–17, 20, 64, 73

endurance, 6–7

Energize Your Teams (Many, Maffoni, Sparks, & Thomas), 6

environments, 5–6

Erkens, C., 28

Estrada, I., 13

evaluation, 20, 21, 22

    accommodations and modifications and, 86, 88

    for assistive technology, 103–104

    goal writing and, 69, 73

    materials in IEP drafts, 39

    in PLAAFPs, 48

    PLAAFPs as foundation for, 54–55

Evans, G., 101

executive functioning, 68, 79

expectations, xii, xiii

    accommodations and modifications and, 89–90

    for parent/guardian participation, 36–37

    writing goals and, 63

F

families, xiii, 4–5, 33–44
    collaborating with, 27
    communicating with, 36, 49–50
    meaningful participation by, 36–37
    meeting scheduling and, 35–36
    requirement to report to, 17
"Family IEP Input," 37, 42–43, 51
fragmentation, 17, 68
free appropriate public education (FAPE), 15, 16, 20
Friziellie, H., xi, 63, 105
functional behavior analysis (FBA), 102
functional performance, 52–54, 68, 79

G

general education
    importance of considering first, 17–20
    percentage of participation in, 25–26
    PLAAFPs and, 48, 50, 56–57
    service minutes and, 94–95
    shared instructional plans with, 82
general educators, xii, 7
generalization, 2, 96
generative artificial intelligence, 103
goals, 19–20, 21
    alternative assessments and, 30–31
    assistive technology and, 104
    benchmarks or objectives for, 78–80
    checks for, 67
    collaborative instruction and, 97–98
    critical questions for, 63, 64, 81–82
    data collection for, 80
    data considerations with, 73–83
    examples of, 111–118
    how many to create, 69
    IEP checklist of, 69
    life-changing, 64, 80
    must know versus *nice to know,* 26, 27–28
    PLOPs and, 74–78
    present level of performance and, 74–78
    progression of, 67, 77–78
    service minutes necessary for, 93–100
    SMART, 6
    standards-aligned, 65–67
    strengths-based, 62–63
    team-based, 65–68
    travel analogy for, 61–62
    writing, 8, 61–72
    writing as an individual, 69–71
Google Chrome, 104
Google Docs, 104
Google Meet, 35
grade-level learning, 2–3
    alternative assessments and, 30–31
    considering general education first and, 18–20
    must know versus *nice to know* and, 26–27
    priority standards and, 28
    service minutes and, 94–95
    standards, goals, and, 64–68
    writing goals and, 63
    year-end goals and, 80
graduation rates, 25–26
Grammarly, 103
Grandin, T., 61
green light areas, 9, 119–120

H

Hattie, J., 27
high school goals and PLAAFP examples, 116–117
home providers, 34

I

IDEA. *See* Individuals with Disabilities Education Act (IDEA)
impact statements, 48, 54
 writing goals and, 64
improvement, continuous, 5
inclusion, 37, 109
independence, 6
 accommodations and modifications and, 86
 documenting levels of, 53
 low-incidence disabilities and, 105–107
 standards evaluation and goals for, 29–30
 transition services and, 107–108
 writing goals and, 63
individualized education programs (IEPs)
 challenging, 16–17
 collaborative approach to, 25–31
 compliance around, 73
 drafting, 39–40
 elements of, 20, 21
 equipping teams for, 1–9
 goal writing for, 61–72
 graduation rates and, 25–26
 importance of life-changing, 6–7
 interventions and, 20–22
 life-changing instruction in, 2, 3
 parents and guardians as partners in, 33–44
 PLAAFPs as foundation for, 47, 54
 red, yellow, green light areas for, 9, 119–120
 reviewing/revising, 82
 siloed vs. collaborative development of, xii–xiii
 student involvement in, 5
 team roles in, 14
 time spent on, 18
 why collaborative IEPs are essential, 13–23
individual students
 collaborating on learning experiences for, 18–19
 focus on strengths of, 19–20
 functional performance of, 52–54
 growth and, 29–30
 life-changing IEPs based on, 6
 low-incidence disabilities and, 105–107
 service minutes and, 93–100
 what their day looks like, 50, 95–96
Individuals with Disabilities Education Act (IDEA), 15
 on accommodations and modifications, 85
 on assistive technology, 103
 families as partners in, 33, 34–35
 on least restrictive environment, 93
 on meaningful participation, 36, 37, 39–40
 on meeting notices, 36
 on PLAAFPs, 50–51
 on progress reviews, 62
 on transition services, 107–108
instructional plans, 82, 94–95
instructional strategies, xii–xiii

intentionality, 3, 6–7, 19, 31, 109
    goals and, 64–65, 68, 73
    instruction and, 78–79, 81
    partnering and, 95–96
intervention programs, 18, 20–22

J

Jakicic, C., 28
job skills, 107–108

K

Kahn, L., 37
Kildeer Countryside Community Consolidated School District 96, xi
King, B. B., 85
King, M. L. Jr., 25
Kluth, P., 93
knowledge and skills. *See also* grade-level learning; present levels of academic achievement and functional performance (PLAAFP) statements
    demonstrating, 18, 81, 89–90, 96
    general education and, 28–29
    goal setting and, 7
    low-incidence disabilities and, 105
    priority standards and, 28

L

late elementary goals and PLAAFP examples, 113–114
Lead Inclusion, 109
learning, 14
    of all students, 1–2, 5–6
    collective ownership of, 19–20
    critical questions on, 63, 64
    demonstrating, 2–3, 18
    gaps, closing, 55
    at high levels, 7, 28
    must know versus *nice to know*, 26–27
    teacher efficacy and, 26
Learning Ally, 104
Learning by Doing (DuFour et al.), 77
least restrictive environment, 1, 5, 8, 21, 106
    accommodations and modifications and, 86, 89–90
    service minutes and, 93–96
leverage, 6–7
life-changing check, 69, 71
low-incidence disabilities, 105–107
lunchbox check, 69, 70

M

Maffoni, M. J., 6
Making Action Plans (MAPS), 37–38
Malone, J., 26, 28, 77
Many, T. W., 6
MAPS. *See* Making Action Plans (MAPS)
Marzano, R., 28
mastery, 76–77
mathematics goals, 67, 79
Mattos, M., 26, 28, 77
meetings, 27
    approaching as an opportunity, 34
    scheduling IEP, 35–36
    sharing information between, 50
mental health needs, 6
middle school goals and PLAAFP examples, 114–116
modifications, 8, 21, 85–91
    comparing accommodations and, 88
    definition of, 85–86
    just-in-case approach to, 89–90
    specifying, 87–88
    using data to inform, 88–90

MTSS. *See* multitiered systems of support (MTSS)
Muhammad, A., 77
multitiered systems of support (MTSS), 14, 20–22

N

National Center for Education Statistics, 25–26
needs, documenting, 53

O

objectives, 78–80
O'Brien, J., 37
Office of Special Education Programs, 14, 15

P

Pacer Center, 25–26
parents and guardians, xiii, 4–5, 17, 27, 33–44
    communicating with, 49–50
    concerns of in IEPs, 40
    concerns of in PLAAFPs, 50–51
    meaningful participation by, 36–37
    partnerships with, 33, 34–35
    person-centered planning and, 35, 37–38
    private providers and, 38–39
    timing of drafting IEPs and, 39–40
PATH. *See* Planning for Alternative Tomorrows with Hope (PATH)
The Path and MAPS Handbook (O'Brien, Pearpoint, & Kahn), 37
Pearpoint, J., 37
performance
    behavior and, 101–102
    functional, 52–54
    present levels of, 48, 74–78
    understanding current levels of, xii
person-centered planning, 35, 37–38, 106
physical education, adaptive, 107
Piaget, J., 73
PLAAFP statements. *See* present levels of academic achievement and functional performance (PLAAFP) statements
placement, 8, 21, 93–100
Planning for Alternative Tomorrows with Hope (PATH), 35, 42–43
PLOP. *See* present level of performance (PLOP)
post-high school transition goals and PLAAFP examples, 117–118
predictive text, 103
present level of performance (PLOP), 74–78
present levels of academic achievement and functional performance (PLAAFP) statements, 8, 21
    academic achievement in, 51–52
    components of, 48
    examples of, 111–118
    functional performance section in, 52–54
    general education teacher input in, 50, 56–57
    parent input/concerns in, 40
    PLOPs and, 75–76
    starting with strengths in, 48–51
    writing, 47–59
"Private Provider Planning Collaboration Tool," 39, 44
private providers, 38–39
problem-solving goal, 67
professional development, 77

professional learning communities (PLCs), xi
　　four critical questions of, 63, 64, 81–82
　　progression toward mastery and, 76–77
　　role of special education in, xii
program reviews, 98–99
progress
　　communicating with families about, 36–37
　　monitoring, 21
　　reporting on, 17
　　reviews of, 62
　　toward goals, 67, 77–78
　　toward mastery, 76–77
Public Law 94-142, 14, 15

R

readiness, 6–7, 28
reading and language goals, 67, 76, 79
Read&Write, 104
REAL standards, 6–7
Redefining Student Accountability: A Proactive Approach to Teaching Behavior Outside the Gradebook (Schimmer), 52
red light areas, 9, 119–120
referral processes, 21
reflections, 23, 31, 55, 72, 83, 91, 100, 108
release forms, 39
remedial classes, 26
reproducibles
　　"Family IEP Input," 37, 42–43, 51
　　"Private Provider Planning Collaboration Tool," 39, 44
　　"Teacher PLAAFP Input Document," 50, 56–57
　　"Team Feedback Form," 55, 58–59

response to intervention (RTI), 18, 20–22
restorative justice practices, 101–102
rights, 15
RTI. *See* response to intervention (RTI)
RTI at Work pyramid, 20, 21
Ruthless Equity (Williams, K.), 19–20, 26

S

Schimmer, T., 52
Schmidt, J. A., xi–xiii, 63, 105
Schuhl, S., 26, 77
service minutes, 8, 17, 21, 93–100
　　determining the best location for, 96–99
　　program reviews, 98–99
　　reviewing delivery of, 97–99
service providers, 34, 96–99
　　input from private, 38–39
　　low-incidence disabilities and, 107
services, locations for, 8
SMART goals, 6
social-emotional levels, 53–54
so what? check, 69, 70–71
Sparks, S. K., 6
special education
　　collaborative approach to, 8
　　continuum of services and, 19
　　Endrew F. v. Douglas County on, 1, 8, 14, 16–17
　　evaluation for, 20, 21, 22
　　graduation rates and, 25–26
　　hard work of, 13
　　high-impact practices in, 27
　　history of, 8, 14–17
　　most significant disabilities and, 93–94
　　number of students receiving, 14, 15
　　Public Law 94-142 and, 14, 15
　　referral processes for, 21

role of in PLCs, xii
the school experience and, 14
shared instructional plans with, 82
students dismissed from, 71–72
special education teachers, 1–2, 14, 17–18
accommodation, modifications, and, 88, 90
collaboration with, 22, 31
expectations and, 31
family communication with, 50–51
PLOPs and, 75–76
service minutes and, 94, 95
standards evaluation and, 28–29
transition services and, 107, 109
writing goals and, 65, 67–68, 77
Spiller, J., xi, 63, 105
standards
identifying priority, 28–30
must know versus *nice to know*, 26, 27–28
prioritizing and unpacking, 6–7
REAL, 6–7
writing goals and, 63–67
state and district differences
accommodations and modifications, 89
benchmarks and objectives, 79
for drafting IEPs, 39–40
goal areas, 64
IEP meeting notices, 36
interventions and referrals, 21
in parent/guardian participation, 36–37
PLAAFP requirements, 48
transition services, 107–108
stranger check, 69, 70, 80
strengths
academic performance and, 51–52
celebrating, 34
communicating to families, 49–50
focusing on, 19–20
goals based on, 62–63, 65–67
in PLAAFPs, 48–51
success
collaborative teams in, 7, 26
how to react to, 82
students dismissed from special education and, 71–72
supports
alignment of, xii–xiii
independence and, 30
multitiered systems of, 14

T

Taking Action (Buffum, Mattos, Malone, Cruz, Dimich, & Schuhl), 26, 77
"Teacher PLAAFP Input Document," 50, 56–57
"Team Feedback Form," 55, 58–59
teams
accommodations and modifications and, 89–90
collaborative model for, 2–3
collective ownership of learning and, 19–20
collective skills and interdependence of, 7
confidence of, 1
definition of, 7
general education first and, 17–20
goal writing by, 64–68
life-changing IEPs and, 6–7
members of, 1–2, 7–8
role of families and, 33
silo settings vs., 2
single settings vs., 2
Thomas, T. F., 6

transition services, 107–108
   example goals and PLAAFP for, 117–118
trust, 34–35

U

urgency, sense of, xi
   parents/families and, 4–5
U.S. Department of Education, 14, 15, 105
U.S. Supreme Court, 1, 8, 16–17, 64, 73

V

vague statements, 75, 87

vocational training, 107–108

W

Williams, K., 19–20, 26
work habits, 52
writing, goals on, 67

Y

yellow light areas, 9, 119–120
Yes We Can! (Friziellie, Schmidt, & Spiller), xi, 63

Z

Zoom, 35

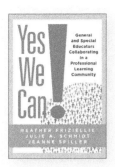

Yes We Can!
Heather Friziellie, Julie A. Schmidt, and Jeanne Spiller
Utilizing PLC practices, general and special educators must develop collaborative partnerships in order to close the achievement gap and maximize learning for all. The authors encourage all educators to take collective responsibility in improving outcomes for students with special needs.
BKF653

The ADMIRE Framework for Inclusion
Toby J. Karten
Create successful inclusion classrooms with a framework that strengthens self-efficacy and equips teachers to be their best in accommodating students with diverse abilities and cultivating supportive relationships among teachers, students, and their families. This book shares evidence-based practices and strategies field-tested by inclusion professionals.
BKG174

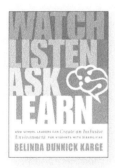

Watch, Listen, Ask, Learn
Belinda Dunnick Karge
Written for current and aspiring administrators and teacher leaders, this book offers action items, case studies, and reproducible tools to help you stay in front of special education law, know and support your learning services team, and ensure students with disabilities receive equitable, inclusive education.
BKG080

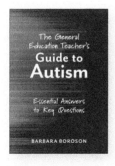

The General Education Teacher's Guide to Autism
Barbara Boroson
In this engaging title, you will find answers to all your questions about students on the autism spectrum in inclusive classrooms. Collect the information and strategies you need to create an effective, welcoming, and supportive environment for these neurodiverse students.
BKG055

Visit SolutionTree.com or call 800.733.6786 to order.

Wait! Your professional development journey doesn't have to end with the last pages of this book.

We realize improving student learning doesn't happen overnight. And your school or district shouldn't be left to puzzle out all the details of this process alone.

No matter where you are on the journey, we're committed to helping you get to the next stage.

Take advantage of everything from **custom workshops** to **keynote presentations** and **interactive web and video conferencing**. We can even help you develop an action plan tailored to fit your specific needs.

Let's get the conversation started.

Call 888.763.9045 today.

SolutionTree.com